ACRL Publications in Librarianship no. 43

The Landscape of Literatures

Use of Subject Collections in a University Library

PAUL METZ

American Library Association
Chicago

In memory of George A. Metz

Printed on 50-pound Glatfelter,
  a pH-neutral stock, and bound
  in 10-point Carolina cover stock
  by Braun-Brumfield, Inc.

Library of Congress Cataloging in Publication Data

Metz, Paul, 1948-
    The landscape of literatures.

    (ACRL publications in librarianship; no. 43)
    Bibliography: p.
    1. Libraries, University and college—Use studies.
2. Libraries, University and college—Statistics.
3. Research libraries—Use studies. 4. College
teachers—Books and reading. 5. College students—
Books and reading. I. Title. II. Series.

Z675.U5M444 1983 025.5'877 83-15511
ISBN 0-8389-3286-X

Printed in the United States of America.

Second printing, November 1984

Contents

Contents

Tables

Figures

Acknowledgments

This study represents the faith and hard work of many people to whom I can only begin to acknowledge my indebtedness. The Council on Library Resources generously provided funding for the project. I am particularly indebted to Deanna Marcum, Program Associate at the Council, for her encouragement and advice. The program that gathered circulation data was written by Sue Guy of the Center for Library Automation at Virginia Polytechnic Institute and State University. I am grateful to Sue and to her colleagues Fred Cale, Randy Powley, and Tamer Uluakar for the time they devoted to the project, despite other pressing demands on their energies. Pat Haney, Mary Hinkle, Harry Kriz, and Jean Thompson of the VPI&SU Library assisted with the designation of subject categories. Their assistance was extremely valuable, as were the suggestions of other librarians who read the manuscript and those of an anonymous reader whose services were provided by the Council. I am also indebted to Walter Pirie and Gary Ulrich of the VPI&SU Statistics Consulting Center for their advice. Karen daCosta and the photocopy staff also assisted with data collection. My staff are to be thanked for their tolerance throughout the project.

In an ideal world, it would not require courage for library administrators to encourage use studies. Since we do not inhabit such a world, I am grateful to H. Gordon Bechanan, Director of University Libraries at VPI&SU, and to Thomas A. Souter, Associate Director, for their support. Dean Gerald A. Rudolph and his associate, Assistant Dean D. A. Waddel of the University of Nebraska Libraries, responded with enthusiasm to a stranger's request for help. Dean Waddel's careful supervision of data collection at his institution was especially helpful.

I am particulary grateful to Robert Broadus of the School of Library

Science at the University of North Carolina and to A. R. Pierce, Assistant Director of Libraries at VPI&SU, for their enthusiastic belief in the project and for their thoughtful suggestions. Dr. Pierce gave of his time with characteristic generosity throughout the project. My greatest debts are to my research assistant, Brad Miller, whose ingenuity and persistence made the analysis much easier than I had any right to expect, and to my wife Nancy for her encouragement, for her invaluable editorial suggestions, and for her insistence that the Law of Diminishing Returns is a snare and a delusion.

Chapter 1

Scope and Setting

Who uses research libraries? What materials are most in demand?
We have few empirical data with which to answer these questions. To
combine them by asking, Who uses what? may then be to confront
ignorance compounded. This study seeks to add something to our ability
to answer all of these questions, especially the last, by determining what
various client groups seek from a university library. Specifically, the
study tries to identify the subject literatures of interest to faculty and
students in various academic disciplines. Generally, the study will treat
these reading patterns as data that reveal the orientations of disciplines in
fundamental ways, but it will also seek to discover to what extent reading
patterns may be an outcome of basic library policies.

The study is motivated by a conviction that fundamental choices in
library administration have historically rested, and continue to be made,
on the basis of untested assumptions about the materials that different
groups of readers come to the library to use. In the absence of data, basic
decisions about the layout of library buildings, the delegation of
authority and resources for collection development, and the
establishment of library units have been based on implicit assumptions
about "who reads what."

On the assumption that patrons who read in certain subjects will be
disproportionately interested in others, subject collections have been
placed in physical proximity, and specialized staff have been organized
into units to serve them. On the assumption that certain classes of library
collections are used by predictable groups whose interest in them is more
informed, but otherwise representative of other patrons' needs, many
library systems have distributed funds to university departments to build
collections. On the assumption that identifiable groups of specialists will

1

use library resources in highly focused and predictable ways and also that their preferred literatures will be of limited interest to others, collections have been dispersed to library units at considerable distances from one another. When we know how close these assumptions come to the mark, we will be better able to evaluate the policies which depend on them.

The theoretical background and substantive findings which have shaped the study's approach come from citation studies and from investigations of library use. The first of these traditions is as closely allied to sociology as it is to library and information science. Much has been learned in recent years about the patterns of dependency among subject disciplines, though not as manifested in a library setting. Vast citation data bases such as Science Citation Index and Social Science Citation Index have permitted researchers to describe quantitatively the extent to which workers in given fields depend for their sources on other fields. Unlike the issue of bibliometric obsolescence or the "half lives" of various literatures, the problem of identifying relationships among disciplines has been addressed only by citation techniques and has been virtually ignored in library research.

Citation techniques have proved their usefulness in delineating the relationships among interest areas on a variety of levels. In studying how small groups of researchers emerge and how their work reflects the mutual influence of their members, bibliographic coupling and, more recently, co-citation analysis have yielded objective evidence of the relationships among individual papers or networks of papers. While coupling infers the relationship between two papers from the number of references they make to the same sources, co-citation analysis reverses the analysis and assesses relationships by counting the number of subsequent reports that cite both of the papers under consideration. In the one case two papers are considered close because they have the same parents, while in the other we infer the relationship from the number of offspring.[1]

On a higher level of analysis--one more compatible with the schemes librarians use to describe subjects--citation analysis has been used to illustrate the relationships among subject disciplines. A dependent relationship between disciplines is inferred when it is found that one discipline habitually cites another; progress in the cited discipline is then assumed to be a prerequisite to progress in the citing discipline. Much work has been accomplished along these lines in establishing the relationships among the physical sciences, while somewhat less attention has been devoted to the relationships among life sciences and among the social sciences.

At the most general level of analysis, bibliometric techniques have helped to suggest larger congeries of subjects which share unique traditions in their approaches to knowledge and are reasonably independent of one another. Here researchers such as Garfield, Price, Earle and Vickery, and Storer have asked more global questions about various fields of knowledge. Should the social sciences be viewed as separate from both the humanities and the natural sciences? Have science and technology each become mature and self-sufficient enough to be viewed as separate areas of knowledge rather than as variant strains of a single tradition? Again, the findings of the present study should be relevant to these larger questions.[2]

In some respects citation studies are ideally suited for examining interdisciplinary relationships. They provide a highly quantified measure of the extent to which one discipline finds another's literature significant enough to acknowledge in its own research. Yet citation studies have serious limitations of their own, which might require that they be interpreted in a broader context. Specifically, it might be profitable to supplement them with library studies or even, as Mulkay has suggested, with more painstaking and intensive ethnomethodological studies of reader behavior.[3] Citations do not reflect in a fully representative way the source literature of any study, as they are influenced, among other factors, by personal style, obeisance to major authors, and a protocol of citing the first published report of a discovery.

Quite apart from the inherent limitations of their data, citation studies can be misleading when they are used to support conclusions about the needs of library users. Much of the citation literature appears not in journals devoted to science, but in the literature of information science and librarianship. Judging from both the authorship and readership of these studies, citation analyses are being used to shape library policies. But from the point of view of effective library service, it is also important to understand the interests of patrons who do not publish, such as students. In addition, the research faculty depend on the library for basic reading and personal updating which will never lead to citation. Library policies should be based on studies of how user groups approach library resources, but the paucity of such a literature has created a vacuum filled in practice by citation studies.

Certainly there has been no lack of studies of library use. A strong tradition of such studies provides a useful complement to citation analyses in providing a framework for this study. Generally, library use studies have been based on circulation records and have sought to determine the relative popularity of library materials according to a number of parameters such as subject, age, format, and language. In broad outlines, the various use studies tell us the same things about what library materials are used. As summarized by Broadus, the corpus of library use studies supports five general conclusions:

1. That overall use is lower than we might think, or like to think.
2. That in-house use and external circulations are correlated.
3. That use is highly concentrated over a small number of titles and that previous use is generally the best single predictor of subsequent use.
4. That interest in materials is subject to a process of (generally asymptotic) obsolescence.
5. That foreign-language materials are significantly underutilized in proportion to holdings.[4]

Most library use studies have been based on the premise that in-house use and external circulation are sufficiently well correlated to allow us to make inferences about all use from the latter, which is much easier to measure. This conclusion has been empirically supported in various ways by Fussler and Simon, by Bulick *et al.* and by McGrath.[5] However, the latter's evidence that the ratio of in-house use to external circulation varies widely across disciplines could equally well be interpreted to indicate extreme caution in estimating the relative use of subject literatures from recorded transactions alone. If the ratio of in-house use to recorded transactions is 1:1 for one field and 4:1 for another, a collection development policy based on circulation data may procure unneeded materials for the first discipline, at the expense of the second. According to McGrath, such variations in these ratios do exist, though they define the extremes of variation and are not typical.[6] To the extent that materials used in-house and externally may differ, of course, it could be argued that we might be more interested in those materials that patrons select for more extended use and reflection at home.

While many studies have examined library use from the point of view of what materials are used, very little work has taken the reader's perspective and attempted to determine what specific user groups want from library collections. Those studies which have attempted to relate patron and use data and to make suggestions about "who uses what" have suffered from methodological limitations. Jenks's study appears to break some ground, but it fails to define user groups except by reference to what is read.[7] In their circulation study, McGrath, Simon, and Bullard introduce the very interesting concepts of ethnocentrism and supportiveness. *Ethnocentrism*--a term drawn from Donald Campbell's description of disciplines that are highly insular in their use of research literatures--is a measure of how much a group concentrates its reading within its own subject field. For example, McGrath, Simon, and Bullard note in their study that 71 percent of music majors' library reading is in class M, so that musicians are given a high score on ethnocentrism. *Supportiveness* is the proportion of use of a literature which is attributed to non-practitioners. The study rated German literature as highly supportive because 99.8 percent of use in this area was by persons other than German majors.[8]

A more relevant definition of supportiveness would focus on the number of fields which draw on a literature and on the extent of such use. As this study will demonstrate, reading patterns are heavily determined by the reader's discipline. For aggregated data, then, the supportiveness of a literature will depend very heavily on the composition of a library user community. On a campus with a small mathematics department and a large engineering school, mathematics might appear very supportive, a finding that would not be replicable in a traditional liberal arts setting. If this is so, any quantitative measure of supportiveness cannot be considered a wholly reliable and stable index of the inherent attributes of a literature, though it does provide one useful barometer of cross-disciplinary interest.

The measures of ethnocentrism devised by McGrath and his colleagues are valid, but by restricting their study to students they have allowed the curriculum to determine to a great extent what is then taken to be a measure of how intensively a discipline depends on a self-contained body of literature. For example, in their study the field of education is given a low score on ethnocentrism and appears to depend significantly on the music literature. The latter finding is almost certainly explained by the reading patterns of music education majors at the university under study. Despite the methodological problems of their data, the work of McGrath *et al.* has gone further than any other library study to recognize the importance of determining reading patterns according to discipline, and to suggest both an approach and a vocabulary useful in describing these relationships.

The Setting

Virginia Polytechnic Institute and State University (VPI&SU, popularly known as "Virginia Tech") is Virginia's land-grant university. Its programs reflect the emphases on agriculture, business, engineering, and other applied arts that are associated with that tradition, as well as the expected emphases on research and extension. Considered primarily a male and military college until the mid-sixties, VPI&SU is now a comprehensive university offering degrees in many fields, including nearly seventy in which masters and doctoral degrees may be earned. The University budget for 1981-82 was $202 million. Since enrollment figures reflect both the size of university programs and the distribution of important groups of potential library patrons, they are displayed in Table 1 according to college and level.

Table 1. On-Campus Enrollment by Colleges, VPI&SU, 1981

College	Under-Graduate Enrollment	Graduate Enrollment	Professional Enrollment	Total Enrollment
Agriculture and Life Sciences	1,756	496	--	2,252
Architecture and Urban Studies	830	226	--	1,056
Arts and Sciences	5,322	670	--	5,992
Business	3,890	315	--	4,205
Education	796	515	--	1,311
Engineering	4,913	632	--	5,545
Home Economics	706	162	--	868
Intercollege	1	217	--	218
Veterinary Medicine	--	--	137	137
TOTAL	18,214	3,233	137	21,584

On most measures of size and activity, the University's libraries rank near the middle of the Association of Research Libraries' membership. Library holdings as of April, 1982 consisted of 1.325 million volumes, with 755,000 titles cataloged. Over 12,000 current periodical subscriptions are maintained, partly reflecting the University's emphasis on the sciences. A microform collection of over 3 million pieces, assembled in part to fill retrospective collection needs when the University grew so quickly to full research status, gives VPI&SU the second rank among ARL universities in such holdings. Approximately 250,000 volumes, principally serial backsets but also books not reclassified from the Dewey Decimal Classification, are housed in a remote storage facility to which daily paging runs are made.

The library system consists of a main library (the Carol M. Newman Library), branch libraries in Geology and Architecture, and a reserve library in Telestar, Virginia, which supports several off-campus programs. A limited number of library books are housed at a veterinary medicine reading room. The Geology and Architecture branches are in the academic buildings serving their respective units. These buildings are adjacent to one another and are within a five-minute walk of Newman Library, while the veterinary medicine reading room is less than two miles away. In general, academic departments vary little in their distance from the main library. No academic buildings are adjacent to the library, but virtually all are within a ten-minute walk of it. Chemistry and physics, among other departments, maintain unofficial reading rooms, which could have some effect on the use of library materials. Newman Library follows a philosophy of specialized services within a strong central library, so that services are divided along broad subject lines. Reference departments in humanities, social sciences, and science and technology provide desk duty, in-depth consultation, and literature searching within these three areas. Reference librarians double as collection development officers, each purchasing for a range of academic departments. Annual materials expenditures exceed $2 million. Until 1981, a substantial portion of monographic purchases were made through various approval plans. A general reference department provides the functions of bibliographic instruction and general assistance often associated with the service role of undergraduate libraries. Each of the reference departments occupies the part of the main building that houses collections in its subject areas.

Circulation control is maintained through the VPI&SU Library System (VTLS), a MARC-based online catalog and circulation control system developed at VPI&SU in the mid-seventies and upgraded to its present capabilities in 1980. Records for University-affiliated patrons are input from tapes provided by the University Computing Center, which reflect the latest data available to the Registrar or the University payroll. Records for non-affiliated borrowers are entered online. Patron records reflect the status of the borrower and, for university patrons, the department in which the patron is enrolled or by which he or she is employed. It is the availability of data on patron status and department which has made possible the approach taken in this analysis. Special efforts were made before the main data were drawn to upgrade patron records so that they would be as complete as possible.

The main data for the study were drawn from a computer program run against the library data base on May 24 and 25, 1982, near the end of the spring quarter. The number of books in circulation at this time was average for the academic year. This program produced an output tape containing the social security number, status, and (where appropriate) department of each patron, along with a three-digit field to indicate the number of books charged out to the patron in each of 81 subject categories as defined by specified call number ranges. "Special patrons," fictitious borrowers for whom records are established so that books may be assigned to such units as interlibrary loan or reserve reading, were skipped by the program. With the exception of approximately 2,800 books charged to these units, the data represent all books charged to all patrons at the time that the program encountered their records. Data on

58,457 books charged to 10,126 active borrowers form the basis for the study. These data were analyzed on VPI&SU's IBM 370 computer using a mixture of FORTRAN and SAS (Statistical Analysis System), a statistical package similar to the more familiar SPSS (Statistical Package for the Social Sciences).

Table 2 shows the subject categories designated for the study and the Library of Congress call number ranges that define them. Although treated as discrete subjects, some of the selected areas could also be viewed as subcategories of other subjects. For example, entomology is part of zoology, and environmental engineering could be viewed as a specialized aspect of civil engineering. The class "VPI&SU" consists of

Table 2. Subject Categories and Call Number Ranges

Subject Name	Call Number Range(s)
General	A
Philosophy	B-BD, BH-BJ
Psychology	BF
Religion	BL-BX
Auxiliary Sciences of History	C
General World History	D1-D893
European History	D901-D1075, DB-DR
British History	DA
History: Asia, Africa, Oceania	DS-DX
General American History	E11-E143
General U.S. History	E151-E900
U.S. Local History	F1-F975
History: Other American Countries	F1001-F3799
Geography	G-GF
Anthropology	GN-GT
Recreation	GV
General Social Sciences	H (unmodified subclass only)
Social Statistics	HA
Economics	HB-HD, HJ
Business Administration	HE-HG
Sociology	HM-HX
Political Science	J
Law	K
Education	L-LD5654, LD5656-LT
VPI&SU	LD5655 (local cataloging practice)
Music	M
Arts	N, NB-NX
Architecture	NA
Philology and Linguistics	P (unmodified subclass only)
Classics	PA
Other Languages and Literatures	PB-PD, PF, PH-PM
English Language	PE
Slavic Language and Literature	PG
General Literature	PN1-PN1559, PN3300-PN8090
Drama	PN1560-PN1989, PN2000-PN3299
Film and Broadcast	PN1990-PN1999
French Literature	PQ1-PQ3999
Italian Literature	PQ4001-PQ5991
Spanish and Portuguese Literature	PQ6001-PQ9991
English Literature	PR
American Literature	PS
German Literature	PT

master's theses and doctoral dissertations by students at the university as well as a variety of university publications. "Government Documents" are those documents shelved according to the Superintendent of Documents classification. Whenever possible, the library classifies heavily demanded government documents in the Library of Congress classification. "Fiction in English" refers to books still in the subclass PZ1-PZ4, a now obsolete classification for works of fiction published in the English language. More recent policy at the Library of Congress and VPI&SU is to classify such works in other classes, and a number of titles have been or currently are being converted from PZ to the other subclasses.

Table 2 (continued)

Subject Name	Call Number Range(s)
Fiction in English (not reclassified)	PZ1-PZ4
Juvenile	PZ5-PZ90
General Science	Q (unmodified subclass only)
Mathematics and Statistics	QA1-QA73, QA77-QA993
Computer Science	QA74-QA76.9
Astronomy	QB
Physics	QC
Chemistry	QD
Geology	QE
General Biology	QH
Botany	QK
Zoology	QL1-QL460, QL600-QL999
Entomology	QL461-QL599.82
Anatomy and Physiology	QM-QP
Microbiology	QR
Medicine	R
General Agriculture	S (unmodified subclass only)
Plant Culture	SB
Forestry	SD
Animal Culture	SF1-SF599
Veterinary Medicine	SF600-SF1100
Fish and Wildlife	SH-SK
General Technology	T, TL, TR, TT
Civil Engineering	TA-TC, TE-TG
Environmental Engineering	TD
Construction Engineering	TH
Mechanical Engineering	TJ
Electrical Engineering	TK
Mining Engineering	TN1-TN599, TN799.5-TN999
Metallurgy	TN600-TN799
Chemical Engineering	TP
Manufactures	TS
Home Economics	TX
Military and Naval Science	U-V
Books and Bibliography	Z1-661, Z1001-Z9999
Library Science	Z662-Z1000.5
Government Documents	Materials classed in the Superintendent of Documents Classification (identified by data base call number convention)
Other	Dewey decimal numbers, any stray LC numbers
Unassociated Records	Item records not yet associated with bibliographic data

By relying on a snapshot of books in circulation at a given time, the study differs from many other library studies, which have been based on archival circulation records and encompass all circulation activity over a time period. Compared to an activity study, a snapshot study will tend to overrepresent books charged to user classes with longer circulation periods. Of course, local circulation policies introduce an artifact into any use study, including activity studies. A one-time representation of circulation records will also underrepresent use in literatures typically borrowed for a brief period, of which children's books are a plausible example. By the same token, data from a one-time sample reflect "time off shelf," an important aspect of materials demand, better than transaction records because the chance that a book will fall into a one-time sample is a direct function of the number of days it is in use. However, the actual use of an individual volume may bear little relationship to its "time off shelf." Especially where faculty may retain materials they do not use for a long period because it is more convenient to keep materials than to return them, a snapshot study may capture a significant share of borrowing which does not represent actual use. With any study based on a one-time sample of books in circulation, the question will naturally arise of how reliably the data represent persistent trends in use. To address this issue, data were gathered again in October, 1982. The stability of the findings across the two samples is discussed in Appendix A.

Users and Use:
A Summary Description

While this study focuses primarily on library use within and across disciplinary lines, the data also make it possible to address the more traditional problems of identifying the library's users and determining what materials are most in demand. Useful as management information for the VPI&SU libraries, such data can be contrasted with the results of other studies and help to indicate whether findings from one institution may be generalized to other settings.

The VPI&SU libraries lend materials to five categories of patrons: faculty, graduate students, undergraduates, university staff, and residents of Virginia who are not affiliated with the University. Differing circulation privileges are extended to patrons in the several classes. These differences are shown in Table 3.

Table 3. Patron Classes and Circulation Privileges

Patron Class	Initial Checkout Period	Maximum Allowed Items
Faculty	90 days	100
Graduate students	90 days	100
Undergraduates	30 days	50
Staff	30 days	50
Others	14 days	10

NOTE: All patrons are permitted to renew items four times. Numerical limitations are not automatically enforced by VTLS, and a small number of patrons have more than the allowed number of items.

Faculty and graduate students may keep their materials longer than undergraduates and staff, while unaffiliated borrowers' book stock turns over fastest of all. Naturally, a book in use for an extended period will have a greater chance of falling into a one-time circulation sample than will a book in use only briefly. Compared to counts of transactions then, data taken from a snapshot of circulation records will tend to exaggerate loans to faculty and graduate students, and especially to underestimate the activity of unaffiliated borrowers.

Because of these distinctions, data on activity are also reported. These data are based on counts of circulation transactions, including renewals, to all patron classes, which are routinely maintained as VTLS management statistics. They represent transactions between July 1, 1981, when the current circulation policies were implemented, and the date on which the main data for the study were gathered. In these data, special patrons are unavoidably counted as faculty borrowers, a slight inconsistency with the main data, where such borrowers were ignored. It should also be noted that the number of potential borrowers is inflated relative to the size of the campus population. Inactive borrowers who are no longer on campus are periodically purged from the data base, but the number of patrons on file is always larger than enrollment and personnel figures would indicate. The circulation activity of each patron class is shown in Table 4.

Table 4. Circulations to Patrons, by Class

Patron Class	Number Eligible Borrowers	Percentage Having Books	Books per Active Borrower	Percentage of Books in Use, May 25, 1982	Percentage of Activity, 1981-82
Faculty	2,541	50.1	11.5	25.0	19.8
Graduate Students	5,572	43.8	8.7	36.2	26.3
Under-graduates	25,518	21.0	3.6	33.0	42.1
Staff	4,017	5.9	4.0	1.6	3.2
Others	3,607	22.5	3.0	4.2	8.5

The findings suggest that the library's heaviest users are those patron groups most intensively involved in advanced instruction and research. Faculty and graduate students use the library most actively, in terms both of the percentage of patrons having books and of the average number of books in the hands of current borrowers. Between them, these two groups account for about 46 percent of circulation activity and for over 61 percent of the book stock in use. The percentage of books charged to patrons not engaged in research or other academic work (and a significant fraction of staff members are so engaged) is low.

Besides showing which patron classes use the collection, the data can be used to determine how extensively various departments or colleges depend on library materials. Such an analysis enables an empirical examination of popular assumptions about which disciplines depend most on library resources, and in particular about the use by readers in scientific and technical disciplines of monographs and other library materials apart from journals. Some of the most comprehensive citation studies in science, including Brown's and Earle and Vickery's classic studies, have established that monographs comprise only about 10 percent to 25 percent of citations for most sciences.[1] Most of the library materials used by scientists, these findings would suggest, will not be measured in circulation-based studies. Kriz did, however, find that engineering graduate students cited the monographic literature fairly extensively, while Marquis and Allen argue that for technologists, in contrast to scientists, books are a more useful source of information than are professional journals.[2]

For the purpose of comparing library use to citation practices, the circulation records of faculty and graduate students would seem to provide the most useful data. Table 5 presents data on library use by these patrons according to discipline. The data are arranged by the colleges of VPI&SU, except that the departments of the College of Arts and Sciences have been divided into humanities, social sciences, and sciences. In general, the results seem to indicate that humanists and social scientists do indeed depend on library resources more extensively than do scientists and those in applied disciplines. But they also suggest that these differences can easily be exaggerated. Neither popular stereotypes nor familiarity with the bibliometric literature would lead us to expect scientists and engineers to be so nearly average in their use of library materials as the present data suggest, especially when periodicals are excluded.

Table 5. Library Use According to College

	FACULTY		GRADUATE STUDENTS	
College	Percent Having Books	Mean No. Books Per Active Borrower	Percent Having Books	Mean No. Books Per Active Borrower
Agriculture	36.6	9.2	47.8	7.0
Architecture	69.1	14.0	65.3	10.4
Business	50.6	11.8	39.4	9.1
Education	41.6	7.2	34.9	9.4
Engineering	51.0	10.4	55.3	9.5
Home Economics	47.9	9.1	50.2	9.0
Humanities	70.6	19.5	68.3	15.1
Social Sciences	69.2	16.3	57.0	11.8
Sciences	57.6	11.3	53.9	8.7
Veterinary Medicine	71.1	9.2	24.8	2.9
Other	40.8	7.3	26.1	4.2
TOTAL	50.1	11.5	43.8	8.7

Generally faculty and graduate students in the humanities, the social sciences, and architecture use the library most heavily, while the least library-dependent groups seem to be in agriculture and education. Broadus's data from a 1962 study of faculty use of a university library also showed that faculty in history and literature used the collections heavily, while faculty in education were less frequent borrowers. Use by scientists varied widely: while mathematicians made limited use of library materials, physicists and faculty in the biological sciences used collections heavily.[3] Drake's data on circulation activity at Purdue are also consistent with the present data in showing that faculty and graduate students in agriculture made relatively light use of library materials, but that use by other scientists was approximately average.[4] The low level of reported library use by graduate students in VPI&SU's College of Education may in part be accounted for by significant enrollments at various extension centers around the state. Also, students and faculty who are on campus use the microfiche collection of ERIC documents extensively, and this use is not reflected in the data.

Intensity of Use According to Subject

Having examined the "who" of library use, one may appropriately ask "what" materials are being used. Information on the popularity of various parts of a collection, both in an absolute sense and in comparison with the library's holdings in each subject, yields more obvious implications for policy adjustments than does information on who our users are. After all, library patrons invite themselves, but the contents of the collection are under the library's control. Table 6 presents circulation data according to the subject schema already described. The first column reports the total percentage of books in circulation at the time of data collection according to subject. The second column is based on a shelf list measurement performed in conjunction with the study. The linear inches of shelf list cards within each of the designated call number ranges were measured, and from these measures, the proportion of holdings in each subject was calculated. Data in this column represent the percentage of the library's collection comprised by each subject. Because for the past several years government documents in the Superintendent of Documents classification have not been cataloged, the shelf list measure underestimates holdings in unclassified government documents. Comparisons with library statistics on shelf assignments indicate that such holdings may be underrepresented by as much as a third. The miscellaneous categories of "Other" and "Unassociated Records" are necessarily excluded here.

The third column represents the product derived by dividing the percentage of books in circulation within each subject (recalculated to exclude the two miscellaneous subjects) by percentages of holdings. The resulting "Proportional Use Statistic" makes it possible to compare the use of materials in various subject literatures in relation to the library's book stock. If the percentage of books circulating within a subject exactly matches the percentage for the collection as a whole, the Proportional Use Statistic will equal 1.00. If a subject is used twice as heavily in proportion to holdings as the overall collection, the score will be 2.00, while a subject used half as intensively as the average will achieve a score of .50.

Table 6. Use of Subject Literatures, Absolute and Proportional

Subject	Circulation Percentage	Holdings Percentage	Proportional Use Statistic
General	.13	.77	.18
Philosophy	1.10	1.18	.97
Psychology	2.50	1.15	2.27
Religion	1.18	2.29	.53
Auxiliary Sciences of History	.25	.57	.46
General World History	.42	1.01	.43
European History	.93	1.91	.51
British History	.56	1.00	.59
History: Asia, Africa, Oceania	.86	1.87	.48
General American History	.15	.48	.33
General U.S. History	1.19	2.10	.59
U.S. Local History	.69	1.65	.43
History: Other American Countries	.28	.73	.39
Geography	.67	1.04	.67
Anthropology	.50	.59	.89
Recreation	1.49	.82	1.90
General Social Sciences	.42	.49	.91
Social Statistics	.35	.37	.99
Economics	7.04	6.30	1.16
Business Administration	3.85	3.59	1.11
Sociology	5.79	3.78	1.59
Political Science	1.59	2.40	.69
Law	1.24	1.61	.80
Education	3.99	3.86	1.07
VPI&SU	.89	1.77	.52
Music	1.17	1.24	.98
Arts	1.99	2.44	.85
Architecture	1.73	.82	2.20
Philology and Linguistics	.31	.38	.85
Classics	.42	.39	1.11
Other Languages and Literatures	.24	.74	.33
English Language	.19	.45	.44
Slavic Language and Literature	.23	.43	.56
General Literature	.81	1.15	.73
Drama	.43	.54	.83
Film and Broadcast	.23	.29	.82
French Literature	.30	1.27	.24
Italian Literature	.12	.16	.74

(continued)

Table 6 (continued)

Subject	Circulation Percentage	Holdings Percentage	Proportional Use Statistic
Spanish and Portuguese Literature	.21	.74	.29
English Literature	3.37	4.62	.76
American Literature	3.34	3.06	1.14
German Literature	.37	.97	.40
Unreclassified Fiction	.71	2.11	.35
Juvenile	.67	.93	.75
General Science	.59	.83	.73
Mathematics and Statistics	4.93	1.87	2.74
Computer Science	1.48	.39	3.90
Astronomy	.17	.23	.74
Physics	2.38	1.55	1.60
Chemistry	1.88	.97	2.01
Geology	1.07	1.23	.90
General Biology	1.40	.99	1.48
Botany	.93	.55	1.78
Zoology	.97	.81	1.25
Entomology	.23	.17	1.42
Anatomy and Physiology	1.74	.84	2.15
Microbiology	.42	.24	1.80
Medicine	3.49	2.95	1.23
General Agriculture	.59	.94	.65
Plant Culture	1.46	.73	2.08
Forestry	.19	.34	.59
Animal Culture	.67	.37	1.88
Veterinary Medicine	.34	.25	1.42
Fish and Wildlife	.31	.32	1.01
General Technology	2.90	1.73	1.75
Civil Engineering	3.29	1.64	2.09
Environmental Engineering	1.03	.56	1.91
Construction Engineering	.74	.39	1.97
Mechanical Engineering	.87	.52	1.74
Electrical Engineering	1.98	1.03	2.00
Mining Engineering	.39	.45	.90
Metallurgy	.19	.10	1.95
Chemical Engineering	1.10	.65	1.76
Manufactures	.57	.58	1.02
Home Economics	1.09	.56	2.02
Military and Naval Science	.49	.70	.73
Books and Bibliography	.32	2.36	.14
Library Science	.15	.50	.30
Government Documents	.94	5.61	.18
Other	.70	N/A	N/A
Unassociated Records	3.12	N/A	N/A

The data reveal a broad distribution of reading interests and indicate that the library is used as a universal resource supporting widely varied pursuits. Despite VPI&SU's land-grant orientation, basic literatures in the humanities and social sciences account for a significant share of use. For example, history accounts for about 5.3 percent of use, languages and literature for 11.7 percent, education and the social sciences for 17.1 percent, and economics for 7.0 percent. Clearly, though, the data provide dramatic evidence of the University's applied orientation. Books in mathematics, the life sciences, and engineering are in heavy demand. This demand is most evident from an inspection of Proportional Use Statistics. Only a minority of the humanities and social science classes in the top portions of the table enjoy disproportionately heavy use (Proportional Use Statistics greater than 1.00); once the science classes have been reached, Proportional Use Statistics under 1.00 are in the distinct minority. Materials in mathematics, computer science, chemistry, and civil and electrical engineering are among those at least twice as likely to be used as the collection in general.

Because they measure demand in terms of library investment, Proportional Use Statistics can provide compelling arguments for the allocation of resources. One possible inference which could be drawn from these data is that the VPI&SU libraries should dramatically increase their investments in scientific and technological monographs, at the expense of expenditures in history, foreign languages, library science, government documents, and other less heavily used literatures.

Such a response might well be ill-conceived, for a variety of reasons. Although they are a concise and convenient measure of use, Proportional Use Statistics may be misleading if they are not interpreted with caution. Non-circulating materials such as periodicals, reference books, and abstracts comprise the majority of materials in some subjects such as the categories "General" (class A) and "Books and Bibliography" (most of class Z). Here one must assume that there is an atypically large proportion of in-house use. Other literatures, such as law or government documents, provide information that can often be gleaned without the necessity of external borrowing, while for fiction, in-house use may be unusually low.

More fundamentally, an inventory of current holdings does not provide the most germane measure of a library's investment, as it does not speak to the levels of current, ongoing expenditures. Proportional Use Statistics will tend to be low if subject collections contain a heavy mix of older titles. They will also be low if collection development policies have been misadvised or if interests in a field have recently changed. Certainly it would be an unfortunate and frustrating irony if a library reduced expenditures in an area on the basis of evidence which really reflected the vagaries of its own collection development policies more than lack of interest in a subject.

The most useful data in determining resource allocations would be use (or even "need," a still more elusive concept) in terms of current expenditures. Thus, neither the numerator nor the denominator of a Proportional Use Statistic is an ideal measure. Circulation serves as a flawed surrogate for use. In turn, use may or may not reflect need, especially in that needed materials not present in the collection will of course not be used. Thus the profile of a given collection will make any use study self-fulfilling to a degree. If current expenditures could be substituted for holdings in the denominator, Proportional Use Statistics would be more nearly immune to historical accidents in collection building and would allow a library to optimize use per dollar investment across subjects.

Most libraries currently lack the data to calculate such a measure, however. While many libraries account for their expenditures in terms of the accounts which initiate purchases, there is by no means a predictable, one-to-one correspondence between budget lines and the subjects in which books purchased from these accounts are cataloged. Thus a library may know its allocations to a fund for anthropology, but not know how many books ultimately classified as anthropology were purchased, either from that fund or from other accounts.[5] Few if any libraries track allocations to the subject classes to which materials are ultimately assigned.

Other, more philosophical objections may be posed to the idea that libraries should try absolutely to equalize proportional use across subjects. A research library is generally expected to be able to support at least basic work in most disciplines. The size of collections necessary to support even basic research varies widely across subjects. These differences have many sources. Fields vary significantly in the formats in which their literature is published, in the quantity of their monographic publications or the frequency of conferences whose proceedings are published, and in the number of the journals which constitute the core literature for reporting current progress. The policies of university presses and other elements of the book trade, which do not strictly respond to market demand, introduce another source of variation. Most significantly, fields vary widely in the breadth of the sources considered basic to their work. Research libraries must weigh all these factors in providing acceptable collections. Their responsibility to furnish such collections is especially difficult to deny when their parent universities expect faculty members in all fields to be productive in their research.

Notwithstanding the many valid arguments to go cautiously in reassessing allocations on the basis of use, any library which finds that significant collections receive twice or more the average level of use, while others are half as heavily used as the collection as a whole, should take such evidence as a strong indication that collection development policies require review. At VPI&SU, collections in mathematics, computer science, engineering, the life sciences, and psychology may well be inadequate to meet demand and may require additional funds for collection development. It is possible that potential demand for these materials may even exceed measured use, which may be artificially depressed by what an economist would call "demand interference"--the frustration of patron demands because wanted materials are already in use. Demand interference is especially perverse in that when it occurs, patron demand is unsatisfied, so that circulation statistics do not reflect the level of interest in a title. Demand interference, if it exists, applies at the level of individual titles and indicates a need for duplicate purchases (or, as Buckland argues, variable loan periods based on demand).[6] Of course, the present data were not gathered at the appropriate level to test the demand interference thesis. But they do show that demand in certain scientific fields is quite high, suggesting that these collections may well be hard pressed to satisfy existing needs.

If the VPI&SU libraries consider augmenting allocations to high use fields, the data also suggest subject fields in which the current level of collecting may not need to be continued. Those fields with Proportional Use Statistics below 1.00 are obvious candidates for review. The extremely low proportional use of unclassified government documents calls for careful scrutiny of collection policies in this area.[7] Such scrutiny would, of course, involve a determination of whether government documents receive unusually heavy in-house use. A possible conclusion of such a review could be that extensive holdings in government documents are difficult to justify, despite their low expense, unless the library is willing to promote access through full cataloging. Perhaps fewer documents should be procured, but more of those which are obtained should be cataloged.

Since the collections in which materials receive disproportionate use tend to be in those subjects that reflect VPI&SU's major academic emphases, it is natural to speculate whether the use of collections in academic libraries generally reflects so clearly the direction of academic programs. Use studies at the University of Pittsburgh and at Bucknell University, two universities with more of a traditional liberal arts emphasis than VPI&SU, provide comparison data which illustrate the degree to which collections usage varies among different types of institutions. Both the Pittsburgh and Bucknell data are based on circulation activity rather than on one-time samples of books in circulation. Each library has its own branch structure, with Pittsburgh having a particularly heavy emphasis on branch libraries in the sciences. The Pittsburgh and Bucknell studies differ from the present study and from one another in their designations of subject groups. For these reasons, it would be unwise to dwell extensively on comparisons, but they may be of some value as a sign of how widely the interests of users vary across institutions. In Table 7, the Pittsburgh findings are presented in call number order as reported by Cohen, with the VPI&SU data aggregated to correspond to single letter call number ranges in order to match the Pittsburgh data. Then in Table 8 the Bucknell data are presented for those subject groups (arranged alphabetically by name) in which call number assignments matched those of the VPI&SU data or groupings derivable from the VPI&SU data.[8] To increase comparability in both sets of data, the percentages of use at VPI&SU have been recomputed after the exclusion of the subjects "VPI&SU," "Government Documents," "Other," and "Unassociated Records."

Table 7. Use of Collections, Pittsburgh and VPI&SU

Call Number	Percentage Use, Pittsburgh	Percentage Use, VPI&SU
A	.1	.1
B	11.5	5.1
C	.4	.3
D	5.3	2.9
E	4.3	1.4
F	2.2	1.0
G	6.6	2.8
H	22.0	18.5
J	3.3	1.7
K	1.0	1.3
L	12.0	4.2
M	.7	1.2
N	1.2	3.9
P	21.6	12.6
Q	2.6	19.3
R	3.1	3.7
S	.3	3.8
T	1.3	15.0
U-V	.4	.5
Z	0.0	.5

For some subjects the intensity of use is similar among the three institutions, despite differences in library policy and structure. The differences that do appear however, predictably reflect the differing characters of the parent institutions. At Pittsburgh, materials in history, education, and literature receive significantly heavier use than at VPI&SU, while the use of classes Q (science), S (agriculture), and T

Table 8. Use of Collections, Bucknell and VPI&SU

Subject	Percentage Use, Bucknell	Percentage Use, VPI&SU
Art and Architecture (N)	4.79	3.94
Astronomy (QB)	.16	.18
Chemistry (QD)	1.11	1.99
Education (L)	3.58	4.23
Geography (G-GF)	.37	.71
Geology (QE)	.56	1.13
History (C-F)	14.15	5.64
Mathematics & Computer Science (QA)	1.74	6.79
Philosophy (B-BD, BH-BJ)	2.63	1.16
Physical Education (GV)	.75	1.58
Physics (QC)	1.04	2.52
Psychology (BF)	3.95	2.65
Religion (BL-BX)	3.95	1.25
Technology (T)	3.99	15.00

NOTE: Classes A, V, Z, and Juvenile and unmodified subclass Q are excluded from the Bucknell data.

(technology) at VPI&SU is much higher. Again, the different branch structure at Pittsburgh undermines comparisons of use in scientific fields, especially since the Pittsburgh data are restricted to the main library.

Differences between reading patterns at Bucknell and VPI&SU are also instructive. Materials in history receive much higher use at Bucknell than at VPI&SU, while the relationship is reversed for materials in technological literatures. In reporting the Bucknell data, Jenks calculated use in proportion to holdings in a fashion virtually identical to the way Proportional Use Statistics at VPI&SU were derived. Interestingly, classes QA (mathematics and computer science) and T receive less proportional use than the Bucknell collection as a whole, whereas these classes receive heavily disproportionate use at VPI&SU. As indicated in Table 9, the Bucknell and VPI&SU holdings in mathematics and computer science and in technology do not vary nearly as widely between the two institutions as does demand for these materials. Though nothing at all conclusive could be inferred from so little data, the comparisons suggest that the collections of university libraries may generally vary less widely than do the characters of their parent institutions and the consequent library needs of campus populations. Fussler and Simon reached the opposite conclusion; within their sample, library collections varied more widely than institutional character and the consequent reading interests of scholars. However, their study was restricted to large universities with world-wide reputations for scholarly excellence and with large research libraries--a small part of the spectrum of variation within higher education.[9]

Table 9. Use and Holdings of Classes QA and T, Bucknell and VPI&SU

	Percentage Holdings		Percentage Use	
	Bucknell	VPI&SU	Bucknell	VPI&SU
Mathematics and Computer Science (QA)	2.77	2.45	1.74	6.79
Technology (T)	4.49	8.86	3.99	15.00

NOTE: Holdings and use statistics at VPI&SU have been recalculated after the exclusion of the subjects, "VPI&SU," "Government Documents," "Other," and "Unassociated Records."

Certainly library collection policies tend to be homogenized by the practices of mobile librarians and faculty, by shared definitions of a research library and the collections it should offer, and by the practices of common sources of materials, such as book dealers. Academic libraries have access to the same presses and book dealers, who encourage the use of blanket orders and approval plans and who send many of the same announcements and advertisements to all. To the extent that library acquisitions are "supply-determined" rather than "demand-determined," library collections will bear a certain resemblance regardless of differences among the institutions they serve.[10]

The characters and goals of colleges and universities vary widely, however, especially as they are differentiated by the traditional distinction between land-grant institutions and comprehensive liberal arts universities. If it is true that the population of users varies more widely across institutions than does the subject makeup of library collections, and if use is as strongly determined by the characteristics of the user population as the data seem to suggest, then we should not expect use studies to be replicable in different academic settings. By showing how significantly the makeup of campus populations may affect the use of collections, the data suggest that the analysis of library use according to the user's discipline may have more significant implications for collection development in academic libraries than would the results of even a large cumulation of book use studies, if these were reviewed without reference to differences in institutional character.

A Note on Circulation Statistics and Total Use

It is a commonplace in book use studies to speculate on the validity of circulation statistics as measures of all use, including use within the library itself. Most studies seem to indicate that external circulation and in-house use are highly correlated, though McGrath did find a relatively large variation in the ratio between the two.[11] A commonly expressed reservation about studies based on circulation statistics is that materials in scientific disciplines tend to be disproportionately serial in nature. Because many journals do not circulate and also because in many cases an article can be conveniently read or photocopied in the library, much use of scientific materials will go unrecorded.

Shelving statistics compiled at the VPI&SU Libraries are not sufficiently detailed to permit a subject-by-subject comparison of circulation and total use as measured by reshelving, but each subject department does report its shelving activity. Shelving of new materials is included, but this comprises a small part of total shelving. The data in Table 10 contrast the circulation findings with shelving statistics covering the period from October, 1981 when collections were moved to their current locations, through April, 1982.

Table 10. Comparison of Shelving and Circulation Statistics

Subject Dept.	Percentage Shelving	Percentage Circulation
Humanities	20.4	24.6
Social Science	31.9	32.8
Science and Tech.	47.7	42.6

NOTE: Call number assignments to departments are Humanities, A-F (except BF) and M-P; Social Science BF, G-L, and government documents; and Science Q-Z and theses. Subclasses NA, QE, and TH, which are held at branches, have been excluded from the circulation data shown here so that the measures will be compatible.

Comparisons between the two kinds of use indicate that they tend to vary together. Differences are in the direction that common lore predicts, with more shelving taking place in proportion to circulation in the scientific and technical disciplines. For the broadest comparisons across subjects, circulation statistics would appear to give a reasonable approximation of total use, especially when adjusted to account for the marginally greater in-house use of scientific materials. The ratio between in-house use and external circulation is almost certainly less stable for smaller subject groupings, however.

Use According to Patron Status

Though not quite expected to be all things to all users, research libraries serve an extremely heterogeneous clientele. Any research library will find that some patrons come to pursue the most specialized research projects and some to consult basic sources in support of course work, while a portion of the clientele comes for entertainment and for practical information, viewing the library as more or less a large public library. One should expect to find that there are significant differences in the needs of patron groups according to their status within the university, or indeed their lack of university affiliation. Before the analysis moves to its core interest in identifying patterns of library use according to patrons' disciplines, the circulation data can be used to examine the issue of who uses what along the broad lines of patron status.

Table 11 presents the distribution of books charged to each patron group. The final column shows overall use percentages as a benchmark for comparison. Comparisons across the rows provide a means of determining which patron groups are especially likely to use materials in a given subject.

Table 11. Reading Percentages by User Classes

Subject	Fac-ulty	Grad.	Under-grad	Staff	Other	Total
General	.27%	.09%	.07%	.00%	.24%	.13%
Philosophy	1.84	.71	1.07	.21	.53	1.10
Psychology	1.93	2.97	2.12	2.47	4.95	2.50
Religion	1.80	.50	1.31	1.50	2.23	1.18
Auxiliary Sciences of History	.51	.10	.21	.64	.28	.25
World History	.59	.22	.50	.11	.49	.42
European History	1.75	.26	.91	.43	2.19	.93
British History	.69	.50	.48	1.39	.73	.56
History: Asia, Africa, Oceania	.97	.44	1.23	.43	1.14	.86
General American History	.18	.10	.17	.43	.20	.15
General U.S. History	1.20	.89	1.39	1.50	1.99	1.19
U.S. Local History	.80	.41	.81	1.50	1.18	.69
Other American History	.27	.18	.32	.54	.69	.28
Geography	.48	.86	.59	1.82	.37	.67
Anthropology	.63	.35	.50	1.39	.69	.50
Recreation	.53	.92	2.68	2.47	2.39	1.49
General Social Science	.53	.72	.07	.00	.16	.42
Social Statistics	.32	.62	.13	.00	.16	.35
Economics	6.50	8.49	6.32	3.86	4.58	7.04
Business Administration	2.50	3.72	5.06	2.79	3.81	3.85
Sociology	4.46	5.78	6.67	3.75	7.58	5.79
Political Science	1.42	1.99	1.40	.21	1.26	1.59
Law	1.19	1.02	1.45	1.07	1.99	1.24
Education	3.12	6.60	1.92	1.29	3.89	3.99
VPI&SU	.30	1.94	.26	.43	.45	.89
Music	1.86	.33	1.47	.86	2.19	1.17
Arts	2.53	1.10	2.64	2.14	1.34	1.99
Architecture	1.14	1.84	2.26	.97	.41	1.73
Philology and Linguistics	.62	.22	.17	.11	.49	.31
Classics	1.16	.04	.29	.11	.41	.42
Other Languages and Literatures	.29	.18	.27	.21	.12	.24
English Language	.13	.27	.13	.11	.37	.19
Slavic Language and Literature	.48	.05	.28	.00	.00	.23
General Literature	1.39	.38	.77	1.72	.93	.81
Drama	.47	.33	.47	.32	.77	.43
Film and Broadcast	.20	.07	.36	1.39	.24	.23
French Literature	.65	.10	.28	.00	.24	.30
Italian Literature	.23	.02	.15	.11	.00	.12
Spanish and Portuguese						

(continued)

Table 11 (continued)

Subject	Fac- ulty	Grad.	Under- grad	Staff	Other	Total
Literature	.55	.04	.12	.00	.32	.21
English Literature	3.94	2.30	4.07	2.57	4.09	3.37
American Literature	3.90	1.12	4.99	5.04	5.68	3.34
German Literature	.32	.16	.59	.11	.89	.37
Fiction in English	.53	.42	.99	2.36	1.42	.71
Juvenile	.64	.37	.85	4.07	.65	.67
General Science	.96	.74	.21	.32	.12	.59
Mathematics and Statistics	5.66	8.04	1.64	.75	1.14	4.93
Computer Science	.77	1.90	1.57	1.29	1.34	1.48
Astronomy	.31	.09	.18	.00	.00	.17
Physics	3.47	2.86	1.28	.43	1.14	2.38
Chemistry	2.54	2.65	.75	1.39	.41	1.88
Geology	1.38	1.32	.63	2.04	.12	1.07
General Biology	1.50	1.77	.97	1.07	1.14	1.40
Botany	1.21	1.16	.52	1.29	.45	.93
Zoology	1.12	.79	1.01	.64	1.46	.97
Entomology	.32	.26	.11	.32	.24	.23
Anatomy and Physiology	2.27	1.63	1.49	1.61	1.58	1.74
Microbiology	.72	.43	.19	1.61	.08	.42
Medicine	2.47	2.85	4.32	4.61	8.11	3.49
General Agriculture	.51	.78	.51	.64	.12	.59
Plant Culture	1.12	1.27	1.77	4.07	1.87	1.46
Forestry	.19	.23	.18	.11	.04	.19
Animal Culture	.35	.44	1.14	.64	1.01	.67
Veterinary Medicine	.58	.38	.17	.21	.12	.34
Fish and Wildlife	.11	.31	.44	1.07	.24	.31
General Technology	2.08	2.54	3.55	8.57	3.69	2.90
Civil Engineering	2.51	4.83	2.55	.75	1.46	3.29
Environmental Engineering	.55	1.39	1.13	.54	.24	1.03
Construction Engineering	.52	.54	1.12	.97	.73	.74
Mechanical Engineering	.62	.80	1.14	.11	1.05	.87
Electrical Engineering	1.23	2.18	2.50	1.18	.89	1.98
Mining Engineering	.40	.40	.39	.64	.12	.39
Metallurgy	.15	.15	.30	.00	.08	.19
Chemical Engineering	.70	1.10	1.49	.86	.49	1.10
Manufactures	.53	.78	.34	.64	.77	.57
Home Economics	.57	.88	1.57	4.39	.85	1.09
Military and Naval Science	.61	.23	.65	.43	.93	.49
Books and Bibliography	.49	.24	.27	.64	.24	.32
Library Science	.40	.07	.03	.32	.08	.15
Government Documents	1.82	.92	.43	.43	.16	.94
Other	1.04	.62	.58	.43	.41	.70
Unassociated Records	2.46	2.75	4.15	2.57	2.39	3.12

The data demonstrate that the appeal of a number of subject literatures varies widely across patron groups. The borrowing patterns of each patron group seem generally to reflect the special pursuits and interests which define its role in the campus community. The circulation records of the faculty show a much heavier interest than other groups display in a number of specialized fields, especially those fields in the humanities which do not support graduate programs. Materials in philosophy, classics, and foreign languages comprise a much larger share of faculty borrowing than is true for any other patron class. Although still a small portion of faculty reading, collections in philosophy and the classics are heavily used by faculty in proportion to what is held; Proportional Use Statistics recalculated to reflect faculty use only are 1.63 and 3.08, respectively for these two subjects. Faculty account for much of what interest is shown in Slavic language and literature and in French, Italian, Spanish, and Portuguese literatures. A separate analysis indicates that faculty comprise 57.4 percent of the readership of the literatures of the Romance languages, taken together. Faculty also contribute disproportionately to the readership of government documents, perhaps reflecting persistence and bibliographic skill as much as any potential to benefit more than other patron groups could. Together with graduate students, faculty show far stronger interest than other patrons in the basic scientific literatures of mathematics, chemistry, and physics. While these literatures underscore many of the fields in which undergraduates do their work, undergraduates apparently do not need the library's primary source materials but can rely on standard texts. Faculty and graduate students account for nearly all (89.6 percent) of the reading in the classes "General Social Science" and "Social Statistics."

Graduate students significantly exceed other groups in their use of the education literature and of VPI&SU publications. Candidates for advanced degrees often consult theses and dissertations as models for their own major papers, and this may explain graduate students' disproportionate use of VPI&SU publications. Both graduate students and undergraduates show strong interests in materials in most of the major subfields of engineering. This is not surprising in view of the large enrollments of the College of Engineering and its relatively high student:faculty ratios. Because engineering has more students in proportion to faculty than other fields have, it is almost inevitable that the engineering literature will be disproportionately used by students. These considerations underscore again the role of campus demographics in shaping reading patterns.

User interest in certain other literatures suggests that other patron groups come to the library with somewhat different needs and purposes than faculty and graduate students bring with them. Materials in recreation appeal disproportionately to undergraduates, members of the staff, and unaffiliated borrowers. These same groups come to borrow the medical literature more than other patron classes do. Materials in the catch-all category "General Technology" appeal disproportionately to staff and unaffiliated borrowers, quite possibly because of collections in such practical subfields as automobile repair and photography. Juvenile literature and materials in home economics are favored by the staff much more than by other patron groups, so much so that for the staff the recalculated Proportional Use Statistic for "Home Economics" is 8.09. The reading interests of undergraduates, staff, and unaffiliated borrowers also show a greater inclination towards fiction and American literature than is displayed by other groups, suggesting again the flavor of public library use.

All of the above comparisons are based on a reading across the rows of the table to determine which patron classes show the most interest in subjects as a percentage of their reading. Such an analysis is useful for identifying the readers of a literature and for showing which subjects appeal differentially to distinct groups. Yet it can also lead to misleading inferences about the reading interests of patron groups. If one makes comparisons down the columns instead of across the rows, it is apparent that staff and unaffiliated patrons read more intensively in business and the social sciences, or in mathematics, physics, and chemistry, or in biology and other life sciences than in the "popular" fields mentioned above. This distinction between looking across rows and looking down columns is analogous to McGrath's distinction between supportiveness and ethnocentrism. It is the distinction between seeing the use of library collections from the point of view of the collection or from that of the patron. The former perspective asks, For whose use are we building our mathematics collection? while the latter asks, What do we need to acquire for the mathematicians? Both perspectives are valuable, but the distinction between them is important to understand and to make.

A further explanation of the reading preferences of faculty, graduate students, and undergraduates is impossible without reference to the disciplinary affiliations of readers in each group. Such an analysis is the next step in determining the extent to which the makeup of a campus population shapes library reading patterns. It will also allow a comparison between reading preferences as manifested in library circulations and as traced through the fossil evidence of citations.

Chapter 3

Faculty Use of
Subject Literatures

One question underlies this study: Who reads what? The broader issue of the relationships among fields of knowledge, which the question addresses in a behavioral sense, has intrigued deductive thinkers as different in perspective as Auguste Comte and Melvil Dewey, as well as the more empirically minded, such as Derek J. de Solla Price. Interesting in its own right, the question becomes more important as science and technology consolidate their roles as major forces in modern society.

Though they have not often asked this question in their research, librarians should find that a number of important policy choices depend on the answers. Should we establish a branch library in physics? a math-physics branch? a library for all the "hard" sciences? Perhaps there should be no branches at all. If we allocate all funds for collecting in philosophy and religion to the philosophy and religion faculty, will they obtain the materials in these fields that patrons in the history, English, and sociology departments need? Can we successfully consolidate our reference services in business and the social sciences? Nearly every answer to questions such as these is based on the respondent's observations or intuition about who reads what, though the question is not always explicitly identified. Herman Fussler has recognized, and stated quite forcefully, that internal library arrangements should reflect existing patterns of cross-disciplinary use:

> A variant of the problem of departmentation of major university libraries is the question of the internal arrangement of facilities in a single library. . . [To] ignore the relationship of physics and chemistry to the publications of learned societies (AS), to general science publications (Q), to technology (T), and, in the field of chemistry, to certain aspects of medicine (R) will only serve to make the use of the

library's facilities by chemists and physicists more difficult. Clearly, there is a very large and intricate pattern of subject interrelationships which ought to be considered in the internal planning of a library, and the disposition of the materials of research ought to be related in some measure to this network of joint use of research materials.[1]

Unless one could invisibly follow a large, representative sample of scholars and scientists, the question of who reads what cannot be answered in a wholly reliable way. While surveys such as that by the National Enquiry on Scholarly Communications have asked scholars about their reading habits, it is not generally possible to obtain detailed information about subjects of reading.[2] Even under conditions of anonymity, responses may be self-conscious and distorted. The problem has been approached most often through citation analysis. This method has the advantage of being unobtrusive and quantitative, as well as the arguable virtue of being biased towards the interests of more productive workers, or those, presumably, who define key interests in a field and are first to signal changes in its direction.

Since library studies of how various disciplines use subject literatures have not generally been feasible, it is natural to wonder how closely the findings of such a study will compare to the results of citation analyses. The findings on other questions which citation and library use studies have approached in their distinctive ways suggest that while the results of the two methodologies might be similar in broad outline, there will be important differences between them. Library studies and citation studies appear to agree that interest in most literatures describes an asymptotic obsolescence curve, and that this curve generally falls off most rapidly for materials in the sciences.

Various studies that have explicitly sought to compare the results of citation and library use studies disagree on the extent of comparability but agree that commonalities exist. For example, Baughman points to a "strong isomorphic relationship between structure of use and structure of the literature" of sociology, while Satariano emphasizes differences after finding that nine of twenty journals most frequently read by sociologists did not appear on a list of the twenty most cited journals. Scales, comparing lists of heavily used and frequently cited titles in science, found the correlations significant but low. Nothiesen, whose study was also restricted to serials in science and technology, emphasized the similarity between lists of highly cited and frequently used serials titles.[3]

Some differences between library use and citation patterns are inevitable; clearly scientists will not cite the materials they read purely for recreation. Other differences, especially those which might indicate radically different use patterns from those traced by citation studies, could be more troubling, but only if the premise is accepted that one methodology or the other will describe the "real" nature of disciplinary reading. It may not be realistic to assume that citation practices and library use ought to be similar behaviors. It is probably more accurate to view the reading of personal libraries and subscriptions, library use, and the highly focused research and literature searching that lead to citation as complementary aspects of a total reading strategy adopted by researchers.

For comparisons with citation studies, the library use of faculty would appear to be most valuable. Apart from students' exclusion from the professional disciplines under study, the reading patterns of graduate students and undergraduates are constrained by the curriculum and will therefore not always reflect the intrinsic information needs of their disciplines. Even the circulation records of faculty should be interpreted with care, principally because in those scientific fields which bibliometricians have studied most, the great majority of use measured by citations has been of the serial literature. Earle and Vickery's important study of subject relationships in science and technology found that citations to periodicals represent 82 percent and 70 percent, respectively, of citations in these broad areas.[4] Circulation statistics typically exclude the use of periodicals and so fail to reflect a crucial component of use. Nevertheless, they do measure the relative extent to which one discipline depends on various other disciplines for important literatures. Researchers may be more or less insular in their use of monographs as compared to periodicals--Broadus's study of sociology suggests that the use of endogenous materials will be higher for serials than for monographs--but there is no *a priori* reason to expect that overall patterns of subject dependence will vary significantly for the two formats.[5] That is, a discipline which relies on the periodical literature of a subject can probably be expected to use its monographic publications as well. Still, a measure of caution is in order where library use patterns are being compared to citation practices, except of course where comparisons are made to citation studies of the use of books rather than of periodicals.

Various permutations of a rather simple output format from SAS provided the data on monographic use. Figure 1 illustrates this output format and may help to indicate how the findings were derived. The example comes from a printout reporting faculty use. Similar reports were also produced for graduate students and undergraduates. The column data in the example indicate that 948 books in economics were in circulation to 209 faculty members, accounting for 6.50 percent of library materials charged to the faculty. According to the row data, the sociology department, with twenty-eight active borrowers and ten members having no books out at the time of data collection, accounted for 2.68 percent of faculty reading and had 391 books checked out. The intersection of column and row provides the following data: eight members of the sociology department had, among them, thirty-five books in economics. These books were 8.95 percent of the department's reading, while the department accounted for 3.69 percent of faculty reading in economics. The sociology patron with the most books in economics had ten items checked out. Data on the number of patrons with books in a subject and on the maximum number of books per patron are useful in determining the breadth of interest in a literature and as a safeguard against drawing hasty inferences on the basis of findings which reflect the circulation records of only one individual or of just a few readers.

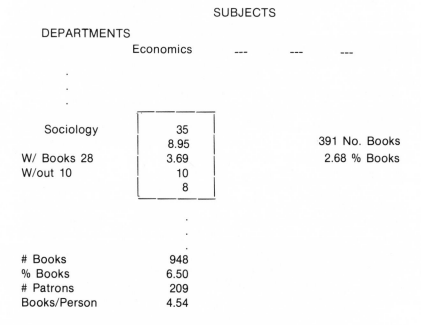

Figure 1: Output Format of Circulation Data

All three reports provide data for the eighty-one subjects, as they are read by all faculty departments or by students in valid graduate and undergraduate degree programs. Because there are nearly 18,000 cells similar to the example for faculty and student reading, a potentially overwhelming mass of detail had to be simplified. To achieve this, departments were collapsed into their colleges, and subjects were grouped into eight broad areas, with a miscellaneous category. The departments of VPI&SU's College of Arts and Sciences were grouped into humanities, social sciences, and sciences as shown in Table 12. For each patron type, data were run first without aggregation, then with only departments aggregated, next with only subjects aggegated, and finally with both departments and subjects grouped.

Table 12. Arts and Sciences Departments

Humanities	Social Sciences	Sciences
Art	Geography	Aerospace Studies
Communications	Political Science	Biology
English	Psychology	Chemistry
Foreign	Sociology	Computer Science
Languages		Geology
History		Mathematics
Humanities		Physics
Music		Statistics
Philosophy		
and Religion		
Theater Arts		

NOTE: Humanities is a broad, interdisciplinary program, most of whose faculty have joint appointments shared with other departments. Graduate and undergraduate programs, some of which are interdisciplinary and bear different names from the departments, were collapsed along similar lines.

Where the tables report reading in broad subjects, the divisions shown in Table 13 underlie the data. Ambiguous subjects such as "Architecture" have been placed in the miscellaneous category, so that each broad subject group will achieve a reasonable homogeneity.

In the following tables, which report faculty reading, data on departmental reading are grouped according to college. Generally, reading in collapsed subjects will be reported, with data reported individually for each subject within the broad group most read by a college. No tabular data will be presented for any department whose members had fewer than one hundred books, though their reading patterns may be mentioned in the text. Circulation statistics for such departments are included among total data for their colleges, however.

Subject Reading and Disciplinary Affiliation

Literature Use by Science Departments

The data on library use by the faculty of the various colleges have shown that science faculty use the library fairly heavily for monographs

Table 13. Subject Groupings

HISTORY

Auxiliary Sciences
of History
General World
History
European History
British History
History: Asia,
Africa, Oceania
General American
History
General U.S.
History
U.S. Local History
History: Other
American
Countries

LANGUAGE AND LITERATURE

Philology and
Linguistics
Classics
Other Languages
and Literatures
English Language
Slavic Language
and Literature
General Literature
Drama
French Literature
Italian Literature
Spanish and Portuguese
Literature
English Literature
American Literature
German Literature
Fiction in English

OTHER HUMANITIES

Philosophy
Religion
Music
Arts

ECONOMICS AND BUSINESS

Economics
Business
Administration

SOCIAL SCIENCES

Psychology
Geography
Anthropology
General Social
Science
Social Statistics
Sociology
Political Science
Law
Education

PHYSICAL SCIENCES

Mathematics and
Statistics
Computer Science
Astronomy
Physics
Chemistry
Geology

LIFE SCIENCES

General Biology
Botany
Zoology
Entomology
Anatomy and
Physiology
Microbiology
Medicine
General Agriculture
Plant Culture
Forestry
Animal Culture
Veterinary Medicine
Fish and
Wildlife

TECHNOLOGY

General Technology
Civil
Engineering
Environmental
Engineering
Construction
Engineering
Mechanical
Engineering
Electrical
Engineering
Mining
Engineering
Metallurgy
Chemical
Engineering
Manufactures

OTHER

General
Recreation
VPI&SU
Architecture
Film and Broadcast
Juvenile Literature
General Science
Home Economics
Military and Naval Science
Books and Bibliography
Library Science
Government Documents
Other
Unassociated Records

and other circulating materials, more than might have been expected. Because citation studies have emphasized the sciences, circulation data on the reading preferences of science faculty should be particularly useful in indicating the consonance between citation practices and library use.

The data in Table 14 show that science faculty rely heavily on the library's collections. Except for the Department of Aerospace Studies and the Department of Mathematics, a majority of faculty from each department in the physical sciences had materials in use at the time of the survey. Materials in the sciences, and in particular the physical sciences, satisfy a large majority of these departments' needs for library materials. The physical science literatures made up 62.3 percent of the library materials checked out to faculty in the physical science departments, while 8.7 percent and 7.6 percent of materials charged to faculty in these departments were in the life sciences and technology, respectively. If the subject "General Science," otherwise grouped with "Other Literatures," is included, 79.4 percent of the books charged to faculty in the physical sciences are in the sciences.

Table 14. Use of Subject Literatures by Faculty in the Physical Sciences

	Chem.	Geol.	Math.	Phys.	Stat.	All
History	8.4%	0.5%	1.7%	2.9%	0.0%	3.1%
Language and Lit.	1.0	1.1	2.9	5.0	0.7	2.5
Other Humanities	13.6	1.6	0.5	0.8	5.6	4.8
Econ. and Bus. Ad.	1.0	1.6	0.5	0.3	0.7	0.9
Social Sciences	0.7	4.0	1.7	3.2	6.9	2.8
(PHYSICAL SCIENCES):	(55.8)	(58.5)	(84.3)	(66.7)	(38.9)	(62.3)
Math. & Stat.	0.3	0.3	68.4	13.5	34.7	22.7
Computer Science	0.0	0.5	0.0	0.0	2.8	2.1
Astronomy	0.7	0.3	2.4	2.1	0.0	1.2
Physics	7.7	2.7	12.4	50.3	0.7	15.8
Chemistry	46.8	6.4	1.0	0.8	0.7	10.0
Geology	0.3	48.4	0.2	0.0	0.0	10.5
Life Sciences	4.8	8.7	2.6	9.8	36.8	8.7
Technology	9.7	7.9	2.1	5.3	4.9	7.6
Other	5.2	16.1	3.8	6.1	5.6	7.3
Active/All Borrowers	31/46	26/40	37/76	29/51	12/23	150/268
Number of Books	310	378	421	378	144	1,768

NOTE: The Departments of Aerospace Studies and Computer Science had fewer than one hundred books and are excluded. Their records are included in the aggregated data for science departments.

Biology is the only life science department in the College of Arts and Sciences; all other life sciences are in the Colleges of Agriculture or Veterinary Medicine. The circulation records for the biology department are not reported in the table, so that the display may be restricted to the physical sciences only. It was found, however, that the life sciences account for about three quarters (74.5 percent) of the 337 books charged to faculty in biology. The actual reading of the department within life sciences falls almost exclusively into five subjects: "General Biology" (18.4 percent), "Botany" (25.5 percent), "Zoology" (4.5 percent), "Anatomy and Physiology" (10.4 percent), and "Microbiology" (10.4 percent). The biology department's considerable use of materials in general biology and in botany is generally consistent with Earle and Vickery's findings, though they found that biologists depend more heavily on chemistry than these data indicate.[6]

Except for the statistics department, all the science departments reported in the table use materials in the physical sciences for more than half of their reading. The chemistry department uses physical science materials for 55.8 percent of its library materials, relying on chemistry alone for 46.8 percent. This latter figure may be compared to 73.2 percent citations to chemistry, as reported by Earle and Vickery.[7] The difference between the BNB classification scheme used by Earle and Vickery and the LC classification used in this study may partially account for this discrepancy. More likely, though, the difference in findings reflects the generally greater use of endogenous materials for serial publications than for monographs, as well as the use of library materials for purely personal reading. The significant dependence of chemists on the physics literature is consistent with Fussler's data (though not with Earle and Vickery's) and with Flynn's study of branch library use.[8] It documents a dependent relationship that others have noticed as well. Storer's discussion of how interdisciplinary dependencies reflect the relationship of a whole to its parts may help to explain why chemists find materials in physics useful to their work.

> As long as one discipline is interested in a phenomenon whose component parts form the subject matter of another discipline (as chemistry focuses upon compounds, the components of which--atoms and the various particles of which they are composed--are the focus of physics), the former is certain to arrive sooner or later at a stage where further understanding of this subject matter requires more detailed knowledge of its parts. Just as the flow from physics to chemistry has been institutionalized in the interdisciplinary field of physical chemistry, so the parallel relationship between chemistry and biology has produced the field of biochemistry and the interaction between physics and biology the field of molecular biology.[9]

Like its chemistry faculty, VPI&SU's geology faculty members rely on the literature of their own subject for just under half of the library materials they hold. Chemistry is the next most cited literature. Brown's 1956 study of *Scientific Serials* also found that geologists use the chemistry literature significantly. However, the library records of the geologists fail to replicate findings by both Brown and Earle and Vickery that geologists depend heavily on the literature of physics.[10] Earle and Vickery found that geologists depend on physics for 33 percent of the periodical literature they cite, or 69 percent of their citations outside geology. Yet fewer than 3 percent of the books in circulation to members of the geology department were in physics.

Mathematicians are extremely focused in their citing behavior, according to Earle and Vickery, who found that 79 percent of cited journals were in mathematics and ranked mathematicians behind only botanists in their dependence on their own literature.[11] The circulation data show that mathematicians, with 68.4 percent of their books in mathematics and statistics, depend more heavily on their own literature than any other department that had checked out one hundred books or more. Apart from its dependence on physics for an eighth of its reading, the other interests of the mathematics department were widely scattered.

Daniel's 1965 study found that 94 percent of the citations in *Physical Review* were to physics journals, while Earle and Vickery concluded that three-quarters of physicists' citations were to physics.[12] As with other departments, the circulation data show a lower percentage of endogenous use (50.3 percent). Physicists at VPI&SU also read a wide scattering in life science and engineering fields and depend fairly heavily on mathematics (13.5 percent) but hardly at all on chemistry. Mathematics is commonly viewed as the wellspring for much progress in physics. The asymmetrical relationship between physics and chemistry revealed by the data is consistent with Storer's theory of dependencies. It also replicates the findings of Francis Narin and his colleagues. Narin *et al.* used citation data to argue that biochemistry, chemistry, physics, and mathematics form a "natural sequence" of relatively unreciprocated dependencies.[13] Except that VPI&SU's mathematics department depends nearly as much on the physics literature as its physicists read mathematics, the circulation data replicate these findings quite closely. In Figure 2, names represent both departments and literatures, and arrows represent reading percentages. "Biochemistry" represents the Department of Biochemistry and Nutrition of the College of Agriculture. Since biochemistry was not defined as a discrete subject literature, the chemistry department's use of materials in all life science literatures is shown, and it is impossible to specify the extent to which faculty in biochemistry and nutrition depend on chemistry apart from biochemistry. Therefore, only a variant of this part of Narin's scheme can be tested. The findings of Narin *et al.* are replicated insofar as the percentages at the top of the figure exceed those at the bottom, which reflect an opposite flow from literatures to disciplines. The data suggest that certain pairs of basic disciplines within the sciences overlap one another in the manner of "fish scales," to use Donald Campbell's analogy.[14]

	22.8%		7.7%		13.5%	
	---->		---->		---->	
Biochemistry		Chemistry		Physics		Mathematics
Life Sciences						
	<----		<----		<----	
	4.8%		0.8%		12.4%	

Figure 2: Relationships among Disciplines and Literatures, after Narin

According to the data, VPI&SU's statistics department uses materials in a broad number of fields. Mathematics and statistics account for just over a third of the statisticians' library use. Faculty members' reading in life sciences may well pertain to life science applications of statistical techniques. Most of their reading in the social sciences is of materials in the subject "Social Statistics."

Technology and Its Literatures

Just over half of VPI&SU's engineering faculty had books checked out when data were gathered. The engineers' reading in the humanities and social sciences is not extensive and falls into no particular pattern except for the unsurprising dependence of the Department of Industrial Engineering and Operations Research (IEOR) on the literatures of economics and business administration. Civil engineers also find these literatures useful. Interest in the life sciences is markedly low. Because the engineers' use of library materials in both the physical sciences and technology is quite extensive, subjects within both of these large areas are individually reported in Table 15.

Generally, the engineers' reading of their own literature (class T) follows predictable patterns. Civil engineers and electrical engineers use the literatures of their specialized fields for about a third of their reading and the technology literature in general for about one-half. Mechanical engineers, however, do not depend so heavily on materials in mechanical engineering (11.2 percent of use) and actually use more materials in civil than in mechanical engineering. Most of the specialized fields of engineering make significant use of materials in physics and depend quite heavily on mathematics and statistics.

Table 15. Subject Use by the Engineering Faculty

	Civil Engr.	Elect. Engr.	Engr. Sci.& Mech.	IEOR	Mech. Engr.	All Engr.
History	4.2%	2.7%	2.7%	0.0%	4.3%	2.8%
Language and Literature	1.4	2.7	1.9	2.9	3.7	2.2
Other Humanities	0.0	4.7	0.8	0.0	2.3	1.9
Econ. and Bus. Admin.	14.0	3.1	0.0	25.2	3.2	5.5
Social Sciences	8.4	0.8	0.3	3.9	8.3	4.3
(PHYSICAL SCIENCES)	(15.0)	(33.1)	(57.7)	(24.3)	(23.8)	(32.6)
Math. and Stat.	3.9	18.3	34.5	22.3	8.9	16.3
Computer Science	2.5	6.6	0.5	1.0	2.3	2.2
Astronomy	1.4	0.0	0.3	0.0	0.9	0.6
Physics	4.9	7.0	15.1	1.0	10.6	9.0
Chemistry	2.1	1.2	7.3	0.0	1.2	4.3
Geology	0.4	0.0	0.0	0.0	0.0	0.1
Life Sciences	0.7	1.6	3.5	5.8	4.9	3.0
(TECHNOLOGY)	(49.7)	(46.7)	(27.2)	(33.0)	(38.4)	(40.2)
General Technology	1.8	0.0	2.2	8.7	4.6	3.7
Civil Engr.	31.8	5.5	18.3	8.7	15.8	17.3
Environmental Engr.	4.9	0.0	0.0	0.0	0.9	1.2
Construction Engr.	2.8	0.0	3.2	0.0	1.2	1.5
Mechanical Engr.	3.9	3.9	1.4	0.0	11.2	4.0
Electrical Engr.	0.0	35.8	0.3	0.0	3.2	7.0
Mining Engr.	1.4	0.0	0.0	0.0	0.0	1.6
Metallurgy	0.0	0.0	1.6	0.0	0.0	0.6
Chemical Engr.	2.1	0.0	0.0	0.0	1.2	1.8
Manufactures	1.1	1.6	0.3	15.5	0.6	1.7
Home Economics	0.0	0.0	0.0	0.0	0.0	0.0
Other	6.6	4.7	5.9	4.9	11.2	7.5
Active Borrowers/Eligible	24/48	22/53	33/54	13/34	26/41	156/306
Total Books	286	257	371	103	349	1,618

NOTE: The departments of aerospace and ocean engineering, chemical engineering, engineering fundamentals, materials engineering science, and mining engineering have been excluded.

The circulation data for the engineering faculty show a greater dependence on the physical sciences, especially mathematics and chemistry, than is demonstrated in Earle and Vickery's citation statistics. Earle and Vickery found that 72.4 percent of engineers' citations were to engineering, whereas only 40.2 percent of the books charged to the engineering faculty were in engineering or other technological fields and over 30 percent were in the physical sciences. The relative dependence of engineers on specific scientific literatures as represented by the circulation data and by Earle and Vickery's citation counts do match nicely, however; Earle and Vickery found engineers to depend on mathematics, physics, biology, and chemistry, whereas in the circulation data the order is mathematics-physics-chemistry, with lower use of biological sciences.[15]

Certainly technology is popularly seen as something " 'growing out of' science, or 'giving birth to' scientific interest," as Price has summarized the common view. A 1968 study of five major technological innovations provided empirical support for this perspective by documenting the extent to which the researchers involved drew on progress in basic research, often in areas with no apparent relevance to the subsequent innovation.[16] The circulation data are consistent with this view in that they show VPI&SU's faculty in engineering using the literature of the physical sciences for nearly one-third of their library materials, while materials in technology account for only 7.6 percent of circulations to faculty in the physical sciences. Although consistent with popular notions, the data suggest the exact opposite conclusion to that of Earle and Vickery, who argued that scientists depend twice as heavily on technical literature (28.9 percent of citations) as writers in technological fields depend on science (14.3 percent).[17]

It is unfortunate that the circulation statistics do not reflect the age of materials being used, for such data would make possible a consideration of Price's subtle argument that with rare but historically notable exceptions, neither science nor technology depends on current progress in the other's domain, but only on more elemental explanations and techniques as these are "packed down" by a previous generation and become available "as part of ambient learning and education." As a consequence, Price argues, "it must be presumed that science cannot flow into technology at the research front but from some position well behind this front." Typically, the process by which progress in a field is "packed down" into a generally accessible body of knowledge entails a codification in textbooks and other monographs of findings originally published in the more responsive and specialized serial literature. This would suggest that engineers and other technologists would read disproportionately in the serial literature of technology and in the book literature of science, and would help to account for their extensive use of circulating materials in science. The available data cannot be used to test this hypothesis fully. They do suggest, however, that if we answer Price's question "Is technology historically independent of science?" in the affirmative, we must accept his codicil that technology may be independent only of frontier developments in science.[18]

Most discussions of the relationships between science and technology are implicitly restricted to the physical sciences and their associated technologies such as engineering. The life sciences and their applied disciplines are not considered. Yet the life sciences embrace a group of disciplines devoted to discovery, classification, and the causal analysis of basic processes, and also a group of problem-oriented disciplines that apply scientific understandings to the solution of practical problems. The existence of large departments in agriculture and veterinary medicine at VPI&SU allows a consideration of the reading patterns of such disciplines, which might properly be termed "life technologies." The College of Agriculture is split into over a dozen departments. As a result both of this division and of the college's low overall use of circulating materials, only three of its departments had over one hundred books in circulation at the time of the sample. Consequently, only about 43 percent of the materials checked out to agriculture faculty are fully displayed under departmental headings. Table 16 indicates the subject distribution of reading in these departments, as well as for the college as a whole. The table also reports the library use of faculty in the College of Veterinary Medicine, which has divisions but does not contain separate departments.

Table 16. Subject Use by Colleges of Agriculture and Veterinary Medicine

	Agri. Econ.	Biochem. & Nutr.	Plant Path. & Physiol.	All Agri.	Vet. Med.
History	0.6%	0.0%	13.5%	2.9%	7.6%
Language and Literature	11.5	0.0	1.3	3.3	2.8
Other Humanities	0.6	2.5	0.0	1.5	0.0
Economics and Bus. Admin.	36.1	0.0	0.6	7.5	0.0
Social Sciences	15.7	1.5	5.8	7.2	0.4
Physical Sciences	1.8	25.3	1.9	8.3	0.0
(LIFE SCIENCES)	(16.3)	(63.4)	(66.7)	(52.6)	(85.1)
General Biology	1.8	10.4	3.9	5.8	2.0
Botany	0.0	7.4	17.3	5.9	0.0
Zoology	3.6	0.0	4.5	4.9	4.0
Entomology	0.0	0.0	0.0	2.4	0.0
Anatomy and Physiology	1.8	24.8	3.2	11.7	22.9
Microbiology	0.0	4.5	5.1	3.6	7.2
Medicine	1.2	16.3	0.0	4.4	20.1
General Agriculture	6.0	0.0	7.7	3.5	0.0
Plant Culture	1.8	0.0	22.4	7.1	0.0
Forestry	0.0	0.0	1.9	1.1	0.0
Animal Culture	0.0	0.0	0.0	1.1	4.4
Veterinary Medicine	0.0	0.0	0.6	0.6	24.1
Fish and Wildlife	0.0	0.0	0.0	0.7	0.4
Technology	3.0	1.5	6.4	8.9	2.0
Other	14.5	5.9	3.9	8.0	2.0
Active Borrowers /Eligible	15/36	10/18	17/29	134/366	27/38
Number Books	166	202	156	1,231	249

NOTE: The following departments have been excluded: agricultural engineering, agronomy, anaerobic microbiology, animal science, dairy science, entomology, fish and wildlife science, food science and technology, forest products center, forestry, horticulture, and poultry science. As with other exclusions of individual departments, their records are reflected in the total data reported for the College of Agriculture.

The data show that faculty in both colleges depend rather heavily on the literature of the life sciences. Reading in other disciplines is widely scattered, with two notable exceptions. Faculty in the Department of Agricultural Economics read more than twice as much in economics and business administration as in the life sciences. The Department of Biochemistry and Nutrition uses the physical science literatures for over one-quarter of its library materials. Chemistry alone accounts for 22.8 percent of its use, as has previously been shown.

The Library of Congress classification scheme is quite successful in differentiating basic life sciences from applied life sciences (or "life technologies") such as agriculture. If the subjects from "General Biology" through "Micobiology" are recombined as basic life sciences and the remaining subjects under "Life Sciences" are considered as life technologies, the agriculture faculty read nearly twice as much in the first grouping (34.2 percent) as in the second (18.4 percent). Accepting this division, one must conclude that life technologies depend on basic life sciences to about the same extent as engineering depends on basic physical sciences. Such a conclusion would again call into question Earle and Vickery's generalizations about the relationship between science and technology. Faculty in the College of Veterinary Medicine read less in the basic life sciences than the agriculture faculty, except for "Anatomy and Physiology." Among the life sciences, the three subjects "Anatomy and Physiology," "Medicine," and "Veterinary Medicine" account for just over two-thirds of the Veterinary Medicine faculty's reading. When the circulation data for the biology faculty are recalculated to reflect the distinction between basic and applied life sciences, 70.0 percent of their use is in the former set of literatures and only 4.5 percent is in the latter. This asymmetry of interest between basic and applied life sciences parallels the relationship between the physical sciences and technology.

Social Scientists

The social science faculty at VPI&SU use library materials extensively. Over two-thirds of the faculty in the four social science departments had library materials checked out at the time of the survey. Active borrowers had an average of 16.3 books in use. The circulation data show that social scientists read broadly and depend on social sciences outside their own specialties, as well as on history and other humanities, for a significant portion of their materials. This pattern of broad cross-disciplinary use within the social sciences has previously been detected in citation studies. The data suggest that social scientists do not read materials in the natural sciences extensively, apart from the psychology department's use of materials in the life sciences. In Table 17, both the broad fields of "Economics and Business Administration" and "Social Sciences" are divided into their component subjects.

Table 17. Subject Use by Social Science Faculty

	Geog.	Poli. Sci.	Psych.	Soc.	All Social Sciences
History	16.0%	10.1%	8.8%	8.7%	10.7%
Language and Literature	5.2	3.7	10.5	7.7	6.0
Other Humanities	4.3	2.3	6.1	6.7	4.5
(ECON. & BUS. ADMIN.)*	(24.6)	(18.4)	(2.6)	(11.8)	(15.9)
Economics	22.4	15.9	2.6	9.0	13.6
Business Administration	2.2	2.5	0.0	2.8	2.3
(SOCIAL SCIENCES)	(34.9)	(32.9)	(36.0)	(51.4)	(39.8)
Psychology	1.7	0.7	10.5	3.3	2.7
Geography	7.8	0.2	0.9	0.0	1.7
Anthropology	2.2	0.5	0.0	5.6	2.5
Gen. Social Sciences	0.0	0.5	0.0	2.6	1.0
Social Statistics	0.0	0.0	0.0	0.0	0.0
Sociology	9.5	12.6	15.8	31.5	18.6
Political Science	2.2	13.1	0.9	0.8	5.6
Law	2.2	3.2	5.3	5.6	4.0
Education	9.5	2.1	2.6	2.1	3.6
Physical Sciences	0.4	1.2	0.9	1.0	0.9
Life Sciences	8.2	1.2	28.1	5.4	6.6
Technology	0.4	2.8	1.8	0.3	1.4
Other	6.0	27.6	5.3	7.2	14.3
Active Borrowers/ Eligible	8/9	15/25	21/32	28/38	72/104
Total Books	232	435	114	391	1,172

No department at VPI&SU with an identifiable literature depends so little on materials in its own field as the geography department. The department's use of materials in "Geography" (7.8 percent of its borrowing) is exceeded by its dependence on each of three other subjects: "Economics" (22.4 percent), "Sociology" (9.5 percent), and "Education" (9.5 percent). This finding is consistent with the observations of Mikesell, a geographer, who noted that for geographers "imports are more prominent than exports."[19] It also replicates McGrath's evidence that both undergraduates and graduate students in geography rely less on library materials in their field than do students in most other disciplines. One should be careful, of course, not to infer too much from the circulation records of only eight active borrowers. The geographers' use of materials in economics and history is consistent with Stoddart's 1966 study of citations in geography.[20] Their use of materials in sociology is consistent with Mikesell's opinion that "communications between geography and sociology has been more effective than that between geography and any other social science." When making his observations in 1967, Mikesell lamented what he then saw as poor communications between economics and geography, but he did point to a recent increase in intercourse between the two fields.[21]

Political scientists also make rather limited use of library materials in their own field. Indeed, the circulation records show that members of the political science department were using more books in economics than in political science, and nearly as many in sociology as in their own field. Political scientists also had a significant number of uncataloged government documents (13.8 percent), which are grouped as part of the miscellaneous category of materials. Generally, citation studies have found political scientists to be considerably more dependent on their own literature than the circulation records indicate. However, the data are consistent with the results of citation studies in that Earle and Vickery found that economics and sociology were the most used external literatures, while Goehlert's citation data show sociology to be the most cited literature outside of political science.[22]

Few departments use as wide a variety of materials as VPI&SU's faculty in psychology. Psychology accounts for only 10.5 percent of their reading. This pattern of wide reading is consistent with Daniel's findings based on citation counts.[23] That sociology accounts for over 15 percent of the department's reading is perhaps not surprising, but life sciences might not have been expected to account for over one-quarter of the department's use of library materials. Many materials in such areas as learning disabilities or neurology are classified in the life sciences, though they might equally well be considered psychology; to this extent, ambiguities in the Library of Congress classification scheme may account for the department's limited use of materials classified in psychology. All the psychologists' use of materials in the life sciences is spread over three literatures: "Zoology" (5.3 percent), "Anatomy and Physiology" (7.0 percent), and "Medicine" (15.8 percent). Based on his arguments about the relationships among disciplines whose objects of study are related as a whole to its parts, Storer predicted that the flow of knowledge from biological to social sciences would increase.[24] Certainly the reading patterns of the psychology department are consistent with this expectation. The circulation records of other social science departments do not reflect much use of materials in the life sciences, though social science faculty may be participating in the recent interest in sociobiology by reading secondary accounts in the social science literature.

Of all the social sciences, sociology has received the most attention from bibliometricians. Baughman and Satariano both emphasize the dependence of sociologists on journals in other social sciences and on interdisciplinary journals.[25] However, the circulation data show that the sociology department depends more on its own literature than do the other departments and is the only department of the four that uses social science literatures for the majority of its reading. Satariano has noted that psychology is the most read literature external to sociology itself, while Oromaner's review of sociology textbooks discerned a shift from anthropology to psychology as a source literature.[26] The circulation data do not, however, show much use of materials in psychology by VPI&SU's faculty in sociology. Bearing in mind that the sociology department at VPI&SU is also responsible for teaching and research in anthropology, the distribution across subjects of their circulation activity, shown in Table 18, is, however, remarkably similar to the distribution Broadus found in his 1965 study of sociologists' citations to non-serial literatures: [27]

Table 18. Comparison of Citation and Circulation Data for Sociologists

	Non-serial Citations	Circ. Data
History	10.0%	8.7%
Psychology	5.8	3.3
Economics	7.5	9.0
Sociology	34.6	31.5
Political Science and Law	5.3	6.4
Education	3.3	2.1

The Colleges of Education and Business

When the social sciences were first taking on their modern structure, it was common for radical thinkers such as Thorstein Veblen to hope that they would be able to support a technology that could accomplish the social engineering of change.[28] Social work, urban planning, and public administration represent the nearest equivalents to the realization of this goal, but few would say that it has been fulfilled. The statement of the British Department of Education and Science's Committee on Social Studies could apply equally well to American higher education: "there are few people whose functions correspond to the engineering or development function in the physical sciences, and nowhere are such people trained."[29] The colleges offering perhaps the two closest equivalents to applied social science at VPI&SU are the College of Education and the College of Business. Neither education nor business has received significant attention in the bibliometric literature. Broadus and Daniel have studied education, but with different results: the former concluded that education is highly dependent on its own literature, while the latter concluded that it is not.[30]

Table 19 displays circulation records for the two departments within education having one hundred or more books in circulation, as well as for the college as a whole. Reading is widely scattered. Even within the large subject groupings, books are distributed across a variety of individual subjects. The College of Education supports degree programs in the teaching of many subject disciplines, and the faculty may require the widely varied literature they use to support training in these specialties. Less than 15 percent of the education faculty's reading is in social science literatures apart from education. Certainly such low use of these literatures does not support the view that educational principles and techniques are closely derived from the social sciences.

Table 19. Subject Use by Education Faculty

	Admin. & Educ. Ser.	Curric. & Instruct.	All Educ.
History	6.8%	1.6%	4.1%
Language and Literature	7.3	6.5	7.8
Other Humanities	3.7	7.3	7.4
Economics and Business Admin.	6.8	4.0	5.2
(SOCIAL SCIENCES)	(58.9)	(55.7)	(47.0)
Psychology	2.6	4.0	3.9
Geography	0.0	0.0	0.0
Anthroplogy	0.0	0.0	0.0
Gen. Social Sciences	1.0	1.6	0.8
Social Statistics	0.5	0.0	0.2
Sociology	10.9	8.1	8.0
Political Science	0.0	0.8	0.2
Law	1.6	1.6	1.4
Education	42.2	39.5	32.4
Physical Sciences	0.0	6.5	1.7
Life Sciences	5.7	8.9	8.0
Technology	3.1	0.8	9.5
Other	7.8	8.9	9.3
Active Borrowers/Eligible	24/52	18/38	67/161
Number of Books	192	124	485

NOTE: The departments of health and physical education and of vocational and technical education have been excluded.

Little attention has been paid to the citation practices of authors in business and management. Popovich's study of dissertations written in the 1960s and early 1970s indicates that business and economics provided about half the source materials cited and that psychology, sociology, political science, and the natural sciences were also used significantly. The circulation data show somewhat more use of the science literatures than Popovich identified but generally correspond quite closely with his results.[31] Like the circulation statistics of the education faculty, the records of the business departments, shown in Table 20, demonstrate that the social sciences contribute a significant but hardly dominant share to reading outside the departments' specialties.

Table 20. Subject Use by Business Faculty

	Acct.	Econ.	Fin.	Mngt.	Mktg.	All Business
History	18.1%	2.5%	5.4%	1.5%	3.1%	4.6%
Language and Lit.	29.3	1.4	4.1	4.4	3.1	6.2
Other Humanities	3.0	3.8	0.7	1.5	3.8	2.6
(ECON. AND BUS. ADMIN.)	(22.6)	(55.9)	(54.4)	(58.3)	(34.4)	(48.2)
Economics	8.3	46.9	21.1	48.1	13.0	33.2
Business Admin.	14.3	9.0	33.3	10.2	21.4	15.0
(SOCIAL SCIENCES)	(10.5)	(12.6)	(14.3)	(18.9)	(28.2)	(16.1)
Psychology	3.8	3.6	0.7	2.4	8.4	3.4
Geography	0.0	0.0	0.0	0.0	0.0	0.0
Anthropology	0.0	0.3	0.0	1.0	0.8	0.4
Gen. Social Sciences	0.0	0.8	0.7	2.4	8.4	1.9
Social Statistics	0.0	1.1	0.0	1.5	0.8	1.7
Sociology	2.3	3.0	0.7	3.4	8.4	3.1
Political Science	1.5	1.4	0.7	2.4	0.0	1.2
Law	0.8	2.2	10.2	2.4	0.8	2.9
Education	2.3	0.3	1.4	3.4	0.8	1.3
Physical Sciences	1.5	6.6	2.0	1.0	13.0	5.1
Life Sciences	3.8	1.1	7.5	0.5	1.5	2.7
Technology	1.5	1.9	1.4	4.9	3.1	3.6
Other	9.8	14.3	10.2	9.2	9.9	11.0
Active Borrowers/ Eligible	13/26	27/45	13/31	17/26	10/25	89/176
Number of Books	133	365	147	206	131	1,053

NOTE: The Department of Management Science has been excluded.

The strong preference of the economics department (which in many institutions would be found in Arts and Sciences) for the economics literature rather than the business literature suggests that the LC classification can discriminate between economics and business administration with some reliability, even though Jenks is correct in identifying this distinction as one source of ambiguity within the classification structure.[32] Most of the departments' preferences for either "Economics" (HB-HD and HJ) or "Business Administration" (HE-HG) seem predictable, except that members of the management department might have been expected to use the business literature more than they do.

Literature Use by Faculty in Humanities Departments

The printed word is the only tangible source of data many humanists use during their careers. Humanistic scholars depend more on books than do their more journal-oriented colleagues in science, as the National Enquiry survey has reported.[33] It would therefore be surprising if members of the humanities faculty in any university were not represented well beyond their numbers in a library circulation study. With only 14.7 percent of active faculty borrowers but 25.0 percent of the books in circulation when data were gathered, the humanities faculty of VPI&SU's College of Arts and Sciences meet this expectation.

About three-quarters of the materials of interest to the humanities faculty are in history, language and literature, and other humanities. About 11 percent of overall use is in economics, business administration, and the social sciences, and about 7 percent is in the natural sciences and technology. It is difficult to generalize about the reading interests of humanists, or even to display them in a single table, as each discipline appears to have a pattern of unique interest that leads it into distinctive literatures widely distributed across history, language and literature, and other fields in the humanities. Table 21 displays the distribution of each humanities department's borrowing across the broad subject areas.

Table 21. Subject Use by Humanities Faculty

	Art	Comm.	Engl.	For. Lang.	Hist.	Hum.	Phil. & Rel.	All Hums.
History	9.8%	7.8%	7.7%	11.0%	28.3%	12.9%	8.3%	12.2%
Language and Lit.	28.8	27.5	67.6	51.1	5.2	42.2	10.4	43.4
Other Humanities	51.5	16.9	8.3	23.6	7.8	25.8	42.2	18.5
Economics and Business Administration	0.0	2.8	0.8	0.0	15.3	0.5	0.4	3.0
Social Sciences	4.9	16.2	4.4	0.6	17.2	9.7	12.6	8.3
Physical Sciences	0.0	0.7	1.2	0.0	4.0	0.4	7.4	1.7
Life Sciences	0.6	4.2	1.7	5.5	3.5	0.5	1.7	1.9
Technology	0.6	11.3	3.2	0.0	7.8	1.6	4.4	3.7
Other	3.7	12.7	5.2	8.2	11.1	6.3	12.6	7.3
Active Borrowers/ Eligible	8/12	12/23	72/99	16/21	26/33	25/30	11/15	187/265
Number of Books	163	142	1,473	182	577	791	230	3,649

NOTE: The departments of music and threatre arts had fewer than one hundred books and are not displayed individually. Humanities is a broad interdisciplinary program whose faculty enjoy joint appointments with humanities departments.

VPI&SU's art department depends on the various humanities literatures for over 90 percent of its reading. Materials in art account for 46.6 percent of use. Circulation records of the music department, which are not displayed, show nearly the same level of dependence on the humanities literatures in general, but with a much more narrow focus. Fully 83 percent of the sixty-five books charged to members of the music department were in music. McGrath and his colleagues found that students in music use music materials to about the same extent as the VPI&SU faculty, and they ranked both undergraduate music majors and music graduate students among the most ethnocentric in their use of subject literatures.[34]

Probably no discipline has a more diverse subject matter than communications. Certainly no Library of Congress class covers more than a fraction of the subjects generally studied by departments of communications. Books charged to members of the communications department are widely scattered, not only across the broad subjects but among the individual literatures within them. "Arts," "Philology and Linguistics," and "Film and Broadcast," with fourteen books (9.9 percent) each, were most intensively read by communications faculty members.

Just over 10 percent of the library materials in the hands of VPI&SU's faculty rest with the English faculty alone. Outside of the humanities, their interests are diverse. The English department reads somewhat more in English than in American literature (26.3 percent versus 22.7 percent) and shows a corresponding slight preference for English history over U.S. history.

Because of its size and disproportionately heavy use of library materials, the English department provides a useful case for considering the meaning of some of the concepts and measures used in this study. Since 67.6 percent of its materials are in language and literature, it might be possible to label the English department somewhat ethnocentric in its reading. Besides being value-laden however, this term is inaccurate to the extent that it implies a lack of interest in external subjects. The physics department reads 66.7 in the physical sciences, a slightly lower percentage of endogenous materials than applies to English, but because of that department's lower overall use of library materials, its active borrowers average only 4.3 books outside of the physical sciences. Active borrowers from the English department average 6.6 books outside of language and literature. The distinction indicates that, while a concept such as ethnocentrism is useful in indicating the degree to which a discipline's interests share a primary direction, it can lead to misleading observations and even judgments about a discipline's lack of interest in auxiliary literatures.

The English department had 1,473 books in circulation at the time of the study, whereas the philosophy and religion department had 230. Partly because of this disparity in numbers, the English department accounted for 21.6 percent of faculty use of the philosophy literature, even though only 3.9 percent of its own reading was in philosophy. It would be difficult to find a better example to illustrate the distinction between viewing collections use from the patron's point of view and from that of the collection: for the English department, philosophy is but one of a number of significant secondary literatures, but the English department would be a major client group for a librarian building collections in philosophy.

In Newman Library, history collections reside in the humanities department and are selected by its staff. It is traditional to view history as one of the humanities, but the data suggest that such a classification may obscure important aspects of interdisciplinary relationships. History shares the perspectives of both the humanities and the social sciences and has traditionally been characterized by a creative tension between literature's sense of narrative drama and the social sciences' sense of the inevitability and regularity with which large, impersonal forces shape events. Data from a 1977 survey of book use at the Library of Congress indicate that the obsolescence curve of historical materials is virtually identical to that of materials in the humanities and is significantly less steep than the curve for social science literatures.[35] However, the position of history among the traditions of knowledge would seem to relate more closely to the questions of what materials historians use and which disciplines use materials in history than to questions of bibliographic half lives.

Figure 3 indicates the relationships between history and both the social sciences and the humanities as reflected in library use patterns at VPI&SU. Clearly, circulation data from one library are far too limited to be more than suggestive about history's place in letters. But the data do show that historians depend significantly more on the literature of the social sciences, particulary when economics and business administration are included, than on language, literature, and other humanities. Exactly half of the active borrowers in the history department had one or more books in sociology (12.8 percent of departmental reading); exactly half had books in economics (14.4 percent). In the figure, labels stand for both departments and literatures. The percentage in parentheses refers to reading in social sciences when the use of materials in economics and business administration is included.

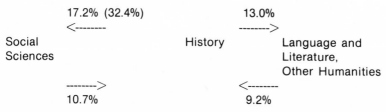

Figure 3.   Relationships of History to Other Disciplines

Broad Reading: The Colleges of Architecture and Home Economics

Most departments represent either the sciences, the social sciences, the humanities, or an applied art dependent on one of these traditions. The Colleges of Architecture and Home Economics are exceptions. The

College of Architecture at VPI&SU has two major departments, architecture and environmental and urban studies. The former represents architecture's emphasis on building design. The aesthetic emphasis of faculty in this department is borne out by their reading of the literatures of "Art" (14.1 percent) and of "Architecture" (30.0 percent). Faculty in the Department of Environmental and Urban Studies (EUS) read these literatures scarcely at all but instead stress larger approaches to man's environment. Economics and business provide 26.1 percent and 6.8 percent, respectively, of this department's reading, while 19.0 percent is in sociology.

Similarly large distinctions in emphasis divide the two departments of the College of Home Economics which use the library most heavily. The Department of Human Nutrition and Foods (HNF) emphasizes the life sciences, especially "Anatomy and Physiology" (11.5 percent of materials) and "Medicine" (17.3 percent), along with "Home Economics" itself (22.1 percent). Faculty in Management, Housing, and Family Development (MHFD) evince little interest in these literatures but instead emphasize the social sciences. Psychology accounts for 16.7 percent of this department's library reading, sociology for 26.3 percent, and education for 7.9 percent. The breadth of the college's borrowing patterns confirms Drake's arguments about the variety of literatures relevant to home economics.[36] All in all, the circulation data shown in Table 22 seem to indicate that each of these colleges is not only distinctive from others in its interests but is quite heterogeneous internally as well.

Table 22. Subject Use in Architecture and Home Economics

	ARCH.			HOME ECON.		
	Arch.	EUS	All	HNF	MHFD	All
History	7.7%	1.4%	4.8%	0.0%	8.8%	4.2%
Language and Lit.	5.2	2.0	3.7	4.8	1.8	2.3
Other Humanities	23.2	1.4	13.3	3.9	0.9	4.5
Economics and Bus. Admin.	1.4	32.9	15.5	1.9	8.8	6.5
Social Sciences	8.9	30.9	19.0	3.9	55.3	23.6
Physical Sciences	2.1	0.3	1.3	17.3	0.0	6.2
Life Sciences	0.7	1.7	1.3	34.6	6.1	14.6
Technology	8.7	8.2	8.5	31.7	8.8	32.7
Other	42.2	21.3	32.6	1.9	9.7	5.5
(Architecture)	(30.0)	(0.3)	(16.6)			
Active Borrowers/Elig.	32/52	23/28	56/81	7/20	19/34	34/71
Number of Books	427	353	785	104	114	309

NOTE: The departments of environmental design and planning in the College of Architecture and of clothing, textiles, and related arts in the College of Home Economics have been excluded.

Use of Periodicals for Research: Some Exploratory Findings

More than half of the materials budget of the VPI&SU Libraries is devoted to serials. Periodicals, the largest single category of serials, do not circulate but are heavily used within the building; the extensive use of periodicals in science is almost certainly the chief reason that the ratio of shelving activity to books in circulation is highest for the library's science department. Because periodicals do not circulate, the VTLS system could not provide data on their use. While reshelving statistics could have been gathered to indicate the extent of periodicals use in various subject literatures, this expensive means of gathering data would still not have provided information on use according to discipline.

In order to gain at least some notion of how the periodicals literature is used by patrons working in given fields, activity in the library's photocopy service was monitored for ten months, from September, 1981, through June, 1982. The service photocopies library materials for cash or charge at a rate of ten cents per exposure. Because invoices can be prepared only if patrons have identified themselves, the departmental affiliation of patrons who charge photocopying is part of each request. In order to identify the subjects of materials, photocopy staff wrote the class number of materials on each request slip submitted for charged photocopying, beginning in February, 1982. For photocopying performed from September through January, and for those cases where staff neglected to transcribe the call numbers, call numbers were identified by searching the titles printed on the slips. Reference books, abstracts and indexes, and periodicals in microform were excluded from the data in order to promote comparability with the data on book use. By these means, 4,680 observations were obtained, of which 93.8 percent could be coded for subjects. Nearly all the accounts to which photocopying can be charged are research accounts, generally funded from outside the university. Because only charged photocopying was monitored, and because the exposure charge is twice that for self-service copying, the data represent a small portion of copying and are biased towards research topics that can achieve external funding. Accordingly, very little information was obtained for departments in the humanities.

The photocopy data for most departments show a greater focus on specialized materials than the circulation data reveal. This difference is due at least in part to the inevitable exclusion of pleasure reading from the photocopy data, but it is also consistent with both Price's arguments and Broadus's observations of citation practices that endogenous materials should account for a higher percentage of periodicals use than of monographic use. Data for the departments of sociology, accounting, and marketing in particular show a significantly greater concentration on materials in the specialized literatures associated with these disciplines than the circulation data indicate. For the Department of Environmental and Urban Studies and the Department of Human Nutrition and Foods-- two applied disciplines for which there is no single specialized literature-- the photocopy data show reliance on the same literatures as those in which books are most heavily used. The social sciences provided 59.2 percent of the 250 articles photocopied for projects in Environmental and Urban Studies, though it should be noted that the data did not capture whatever use this department may have made of periodicals in "Architecture," where materials would have been copied in the branch library. Periodicals in the life sciences, especially "Anatomy and Physiology" and "Medicine," provided 62.8 percent of the 312 articles photocopied for the Department of Human Nutrition and Foods, which is consistent with the interests their circulation records reveal.

A number of departments in the life sciences used the photocopy service extensively. The data for these departments resemble the circulation data in showing that materials in the basic life sciences are heavily used by disciplines in both the basic and the applied life sciences. Materials in "General Biology" (subclass QH) have a particularly broad appeal, as they are used by biologists and by applied life scientists working with both plants and animals. Of the 236 articles photocopied for the biology department, 33.5 percent were in "General Biology" and 25.4 percent were in "Anatomy and Physiology." The department requested copies of only sixteen articles in applied life sciences, which also accounted for a low percentage of its circulating materials. The life sciences provided over three-quarters of copied materials for each of the departments in agriculture which used the service extensively, biochemistry and nutrition, entomology, and plant pathology and physiology. The subject "Plant Culture" accounted for 8.1 percent of the entomologists' copies and 30.0 percent of the copies for the Department of Plant Pathology and Physiology, but otherwise these departments relied heavily on more basic life sciences. Requests from the College of Veterinary Medicine showed strong interest in "Anatomy and Physiology" (16.7 percent), "Medicine" (28.5 percent), and "Veterinary Medicine" (17.0 percent), the three literatures that comprised the lion's share of their book use, but significant use was also made of periodicals in "General Biology" (9.6 percent) and "Microbiology" (18.3 percent).

In very general terms, the photocopy data seem to replicate the circulation data in identifying literatures of interest to those disciplines for which sufficient data are available. However, photocopy records do show a more narrow concentration of use on materials in core literatures. The size of the sample and the bias in the data make further generalizations difficult and any final conclusions impossible, of course. It is unfortunate that library studies have not been able to show precisely how the increasingly extensive and important serial literature is used. The failure to obtain such data is easily understood, however, because only expensive, cumbersome, and obtrusive surveys could fully record periodicals use according to patrons' levels and disciplines. Possibly data gathered in a closed-stack library can realize this goal. Of course, photocopy data are easily obtained and may be less biased in an institution where all photocopying is centralized or where rates are not greater for photocopy service than for self-service copying, but first it would be necessary to determine how well photocopy activity represents all use of periodicals. Data from the Pittsburgh study indicate that only about one-quarter of articles read in libraries are photocopied; it would be essential, before photocopy data can be trusted as an index of periodicals use, to know how well they represent the remaining three-quarters of library use of these materials.[37]

Literature Use by Nonspecialists

Many librarians categorize subject literatures according to whether they are highly specialized or widely popular. The belief that most literatures in the humanities and social sciences are heavily read by nonspecialists has been a strong factor in exempting these fields from pressures to build branch libraries. References to the breadth of appeal of various literatures are common in the citation literature. For example, Brown refers to chemistry as broadly supportive of a variety of scientific disciplines, while Earle and Vickery's analysis of social science literatures concluded that materials in education and political science are of limited value to nonspecialists.[38]

While on its face a simple concept, the idea that literatures vary in how widely they appeal to different groups of readers presents nearly insuperable problems of definition and measurement. Intuitively we feel that the "suportiveness" of a literature, to use McGrath's term, should reflect its overall popularity; otherwise a little-read literature could qualify as highly supportive of other disciplines simply because few of its readers were from a discipline considered to be closely related. Yet popularity depends greatly on how widely or narrowly literatures are defined. If we break history into twenty specialized literatures, we will certainly find that no one of them accounts for a significant share of use, but all of history taken together will be used extensively. Other problems of definition confuse the issue. By its nature supportiveness rests on an explicit matching of disciplines and their literatures, a subjective judgment in any event and one which often involves arbitrary choices among equally sensible alternatives. For example, either all engineers or only mechanical engineers could be considered the natural readership for materials in mechanical engineering. The more narrowly its readership group is defined, the more supportive a given literature will appear to be.

Many scientists hold that a concept which cannot be defined in a way that facilitates measurement (or "operationalized") has no meaning. The choice with supportiveness seems, then, to be one between using a flawed measure or discarding a concept that provides a useful way of approaching library use from a collection's point of view. Probably there is no better approach to the question of how widely a subject literature is read than McGrath's operationalization of supportiveness in terms of the percentage of a literature's readers who fall outside its natural

Table 23. Supportiveness Scores of Literatures

Literature	Proportion Reading Not by Reader Group	Reader Group	Overall Faculty Reading Percentage
Psychology	.96	Psychology Dept.	1.93
Religion	.94	Philosophy and Religion Dept.	1.80
History	.84	History Dept.	6.94
General Science	.81	Agriculture, Science Depts.	0.96
Sociology	.81	Sociology Dept.	4.46
Music	.80	Music Dept.	1.86
Art	.79	Art Dept.	2.53
Philosophy	.75	Philosophy and Religion Dept.	1.84
Geography	.74	Geography Dept.	0.48
Political Science	.72	Political Science Dept.	1.42
Chemical Engineering	.72	Engineering College	0.70
Computer Science	.72	Computer Science Dept.	0.77
Home Economics	.71	Home Economics College	0.57
Medicine	.69	Colleges of Agriculture and Veterinary Medicine, Biology Dept.	2.47
Education	.66	Education College	3.12
Physics	.63	Physics Dept.	3.47
Chemistry	.61	Chemistry Dept.	2.54
Mathematics and Statistics	.59	Mathematics and Statistics Depts.	5.66
Business Administration	.57	Business College	2.50
Mining Engineering	.56	Engineering College	0.40
Other Languages	.55	Humanities Depts.	0.29
Animal Culture	.53	Colleges of Agriculture and Veterinary Medicine	0.35
Library Science	.51	Library faculty	0.40
Environmental Engineering	.51	Colleges of Architecture and Engineering	055 0.55
Zoology	.48	Colleges of Agriculture and Veterinary Medicine, Biology Dept.	1.12

constituency.[39] When such a definition of supportiveness is applied, peculiarities in the makeup of the population under study will inevitably influence findings and make them less generalizable, although for the librarians in any given system, generalizability is of little or no concern, and it is inherently valuable to discover how much each literature is read by nonspecialists. If special conditions are fully reported, statistics on supportiveness become more useful to others, as well.

In Table 23, supportiveness is defined for each subject literature that appears to have a natural client group. The second column reports the percentage of reading in each subject which is attributable to faculty apart from the natural reading group, as this is defined in the third column. So that overall subject popularity is not omitted from consideration, the percentage of faculty borrowing associated with each literature is reported in the fourth column. For the first subject listed, "Psychology," the data indicate that faculty from outside the psychology department account for 96 percent of faculty reading, and that 1.93

Table 23 (continued)

Literature	Proportion Reading Not by Reader Group	Reader Group	Overall Faculty Reading Percentage
Forestry	.48	Agriculture College	0.19
Plant Culture	.47	Agriculture College	1.12
Construction Engineering	.46	Colleges of Architecture and Engineering	0.52
German Literature	.43	Humanities Depts.	0.32
American Literature	.41	English Dept.	3.90
Electrical Engineering	.37	Engineering College	1.23
General Biology	.37	Colleges of Agriculture and Veterinary Medicine Biology Dept.	1.50
English Literature	.33	English Dept.	3.94
Mechanical Engineering	.29	Engineering College	0.62
Anatomy and Physiology	.29	Colleges of Agriculture and Veterinary Medicine, Biology Dept.	2.27
Veterinary Medicine	.29	Veterinary Medicine	0.58
Civil Engineering	.24	Engineering College	2.51
Architecture	.22	Architecture College	1.14
French Literature	.17	Humanities Depts.	0.65
Spanish and Portuguese Literature	.14	Humanities Depts.	0.55
Botany	.11	College of Agriculture, Biology Dept.	1.21
Geology	.09	Geology Dept.	1.38
Microbiology	.08	Colleges of Agriculture, Veterinary Medicine, Biology Dept.	0.72
Italian Literature	.06	Humanities Depts.	0.23
Classics	.02	Humanities Depts.	1.16

percent of overall faculty reading is in psychology. Rough comparisons of the extent of nonspecialist reading can be facilitated by calculating the products of the second and fourth columns for the various literatures.

The findings consist partly of artifacts reflecting local conditions only and partly of what appear to be valid and substantively useful results. Unquestionably history and medicine would appear to be less supportive if VPI&SU had a larger history department or a medical school, while English and American literature would be read more by outsiders if the University's other humanities departments were as large in proportion to English as they are in most liberal arts universities. Supportiveness scores depend not only on the population of potential readers from outside a specialty, but also on the interests of specialists. "Psychology" would have a lower score if VPI&SU's department relied on the psychology literature for more than 10.5 percent of its reading, a percentage which might well reflect an unusual orientation of the department at VPI&SU. Yet the high score for "Psychology" is also attributable to rather substantial interest in its literature shown by faculty in other departments, including the departments of marketing and of management, housing, and family development and the College of Education. Sociology is an important literature to the College of Education and to the departments of environmental and urban studies, of marketing, of management, housing, and family development, and to those of geography, political science, and psychology; its supportiveness score accurately reflects the value of this literature to external disciplines and replicates Earle and Vickery's findings about the utility of materials in sociology to researchers in other disciplines. At the other extreme, nearly any mode of calculation will show that materials in "Geology" and "Classics" are of negligible interest to faculty in most external departments. The low supportiveness scores for these literatures do not seem to be attributable simply to demographic peculiarities of VPI&SU.

As with findings that reflect the reader's point of view, the most general statements supported by the data are those that could most confidently be expected to be replicable in other settings. The most general statement the data support is also the most important, especially for its implications for library policies. The data show quite clearly that the majority of faculty use of most subject literatures is by outsiders--that is, by readers with other specialties than those primarily associated with those literatures. The findings support a view of the library as a most unrestricted and unpredictable bazaar for the exchange of ideas and reflect a much more catholic and interdependent view of knowledge than citation studies have ever suggested. This view of library use, in turn, suggests policies stressing the integration of services, an opposition to arbitrary barriers to the flow of information, and the avoidance of narrow specialization.

Table 24 gives the readership of each broad subject category, according to colleges. This table differs from previous tables in that data in each column report the readership of a literature, rather than literatures read by a specified department or college. Naturally the findings show less external reading than do data for individual departments, but the degree to which patrons from outside even the colleges most associated with broad literatures make use of their materials further illustrates the extent of cross-disciplinary library use. For example, only a minority of faculty reading in "History" is by faculty in humanities departments, while the College of Business accounts for less than 40 percent of all faculty use in "Economics and Business Administration." If Veterinary Medicine, the smallest college, is excluded, there are no "empy cells" in the table: someone from every other college has materials in each broad subject. In fact, examination of the data on the number of active borrowers reveals that at least three faculty members from every college except Veterinary Medicine have books in each broad subject. "Never say never" would appear to be the byword governing statements about who does or does not read what.

Table 24. Readership of Broad Subject Literatures

Readers	Hist.	Lang. & Lit.	Other Hum.	Econ. & Bus. Adm.	Soc. Sci.	Phys. Sci.	Life Sci.	Tech.
Agriculture	3.6%	1.9%	1.5%	7.0%	4.3%	4.9%	35.6%	7.6%
Architecture	3.8	1.4	8.9	9.3	7.3	0.5	0.6	4.7
Business	4.7	3.0	2.3	38.7	8.2	2.6	1.5	2.6
Education	2.0	1.8	3.1	1.9	11.1	0.4	2.1	3.2
Engineering	4.5	1.6	2.7	6.8	3.4	25.5	2.6	45.2
Home Econ.	1.3	0.3	1.2	1.5	3.6	0.9	2.5	7.0
Humanities	44.0	74.1	57.6	8.2	14.8	3.0	3.9	9.4
Social Sciences	12.3	3.3	4.5	14.2	22.7	0.5	4.2	1.1
Sciences	6.1	2.4	7.3	1.4	2.8	54.9	22.2	9.9
Vet. Med.	1.9	0.3	0.0	0.0	0.1	0.0	11.7	0.4
Other	15.8	9.8	10.9	11.0	21.8	6.7	13.1	9.0

NOTE: Other faculty account for 13.3 percent of faculty reading, or 9.2 percent after library faculty have been excluded. Administrators and extension agents account for many of the "Other" faculty.

The supportiveness scores for the various literatures demonstrate rather broad patterns of reading across disciplinary lines. The analysis of data on the number of patrons who borrow materials in given literatures can help further to specify dependent relationships and to show just how crucial cross-disciplinary reading is. Most patrons seem to borrow the highest number of materials in their specialties, supplementing these interests with broad but less deep interests in other literatures. Circulation records for most departments reflect a pattern of intensive interest in the subjects closest to home, as measured by the mean number of books per active borrower, together with a tapering off to more eclectic and shallow interests for less immediately relevant subjects. The pattern emerges most clearly when both departments and subjects are aggregated, giving more stability to measures of mean numbers of books per patron. Table 25 demonstrates the strong differences in mean number of books in each of the eight major fields per active borrower for faculty in all departments of the colleges of architecture, business, and arts and sciences. Scores within each cell of the table reflect the mean number of books in a broad field charged to active faculty borrowers of those literatures from the college or branch of Arts and Sciences indicated by the row heading. Because in each case only active borrowers of a specific subject literature are represented, the table does not simply restate the fact that departments read most heavily in their own literatures. Instead, it shows that even where individuals use materials in other literatures, their interest in them is typically less intensive.

Table 25. Mean Number of Books per Active Borrower

	Hist.	Lang. & Lit.	Other Hum.	Econ. & Bus. Ad.	Soc. Sci.	Phys. Sci.	Life Sci.	Tech.	Other
Agriculture	3.3	3.1	2.0	5.8	3.1	4.4	7.0	2.8	2.7
Business	4.8	3.8	1.9	7.5	3.9	2.8	2.8	2.2	3.6
Humanities	5.6	12.7	7.3	4.0	4.1	4.7	2.8	4.8	3.0
Social Sci.	4.5	3.3	3.5	6.9	8.3	1.8	3.3	2.3	6.0
Sciences	3.0	2.5	5.7	1.4	2.0	8.3	5.6	3.1	2.6

Patrons from more remote disciplines who use materials in a given literature routinely borrow fewer books than do patrons from fields which traditionally rely on that literature. Typically, then, the readership of a literature will consist of a small core of heavy users from closely related disciplines and a large number of patrons from more distant fields who borrow a limited number of materials. As a consequence, the proportion of patrons from outside the natural readership of a literature, however this is defined, will almost always exceed the proportion of books in the hands of outsiders. Table 26 compares the percentage of books in the hands of nonspecialists for each of the major subject groups to the percentage of nonspecialists among active borrowers of these literatures. In each case, the latter percentage is larger. As significant as the volume of cross-disciplinary reading appears when books are the unit of analysis, the traffic across disciplinary lines is even more dramatically evident when patrons are considered.

Table 26. Percentage of External Borrowing and Patrons

Literature	Native Group	Percentage of Books to Outside Borrowers	Percentage Outside Borrowers
History	Humanities	56.0	66.4
Lang. and Lit.	Humanities	25.9	59.2
Other Humanities	Humanities	42.4	61.4
Economics and Bus. Admin.	Business	61.3	74.4
Social Sciences	Social Sci.	77.3	87.2
Physical Sciences	Science and Engineering	19.5	33.4
Life Sciences	Agriculture, Vet. Med., Biol. Dept.	39.0	58.0
Technology	Engineering	54.8	69.0

Some Implications for Collection Development

The data have shown that nonspecialists account for a large share of the use of most subject literatures and that outside persons who use a literature outnumber specialists even more dramatically. Since collections are used so heavily by outsiders, it is natural to wonder whether they approach literatures in the same way and with the same goals as specialists. Quite possibly outsiders seek a somewhat older, more approachable literature which makes accessible to them more basic understandings they need for their work--in short, materials that have been "packed down" for general understanding, in Price's phrase.

The issue of whether specialists and nonspecialists approach subject literatures similarly is of more than idle interest. In many academic libraries, especially college libraries, academic departments are allocated funds for the purchase of all or most library materials. This practice has been criticized on many grounds, among them the fear that strong individuals with idiosyncratic tastes may build collections that do not represent a department's real current and future needs.[40] The data suggest the possibility of a larger danger, that the approach of an entire academic department to its primary literatures may be fundamentally different from the approach of nonspecialists, so much so that a collection which satisfies the department may frustrate other readers. Unfortunately, many older bibliographic records in the data base do not contain data on format, age, or language, making it impossible to compare use by specialists and nonspecialists in terms of these parameters. However, for a number of cases where individual departments could be presumed to have a primary interest in several subject literatures, it is possible to compare the distribution of departmental interests across those subjects with the interests of other faculty, as well as those of non-faculty readers. If differences in these distributions are large, and if we can assume that departments entrusted to build collections will generally purchase materials that reflect their own definitions of their fields, then fund allocation must be considered suspect on the grounds that important reading groups' needs for library materials will be poorly represented. The high degree of cross-disciplinary reading which the data indicate make it all the more important that library collections serve the needs of "outside" readers.

Tables 27 through 32 compare the reading interests of faculty in five departments and the College of Engineering to the interests of other faculty, and then to the circulation records of all non-faculty patrons. Chi-square tests are used to determine the statistical significance of differences. The chi-square tests are useful for indicating the presence of a non-random relationship--certainly if chi-square is not statistically significant the distribution of two groups' circulation activity across subjects should be considered indistinguishable--but they should be interpreted with great caution. Properly speaking, chi-square should be applied only when measures are independent, which is manifestly not true when a single individual's interests can account for dozens of observations. In other words, the large number of books in "Philosophy" and "Religion" charged to the faculty of the philosophy and religion department should not obscure the fact that the department has only eleven active borrowers, one or two of whom can significantly affect the findings. Especially when only a general difference of reading interests has been predicted, rather than a testable direction of difference, the chi-square statistics must be considered merely indicative, not conclusive. Any conclusion that departments typically approach their subject literatures in an unrepresentative manner must be based on an overall impression of the extent of differences in all six tables.

Table 27. Reading Interests in English and American Literature

Subject	Engl. Faculty	Other Faculty	Other Patrons
English Language	6 (0.8%)	13 (2.6%)	91 (2.8%)
English Literature	388 (52.2)	187 (37.6)	1,397 (43.5)
American Literature	334 (45.0)	235 (47.2)	1,386 (43.2)
Unreclassified Fiction	15 (2.0)	63 (12.7)	337 (10.5)

Cols. 1 & 2: chi-square=74.13, 3 d.f., p<.001
Cols. 1 & 3: chi-square=69.39, 3 d.f., p<.001

Table 28. Reading Interests in Philosophy and Religion

Subject	Philo. & Religion Faculty	Other Faculty	Other Patrons
Philosophy	66 (81.5%)	203 (45.1%)	373 (46.6%)
Religion	15 (18.5)	247 (54.9)	428 (53.4)

Cols. 1 & 2: chi-square=36.33, 1 d.f., p<.001
Cols. 1 & 3: chi-square=35.87, 1 d.f., p<.001

Table 29. Reading Interests in Sociology and Anthropology

Subject	Sociology Faculty	Other Faculty	Other Patrons
Anthropology	22 (15.2%)	70 (11.7%)	200 (6.8%)
Sociology	123 (84.8)	528 (88.3)	2,733 (93.2)

Cols. 1 & 2: chi-square= 1.29, 1 d.f., n.s.
Cols. 1 & 3: chi-square=14.41, 1 d.f., p<.001

Table 30. Reading Interests in History

Subject	History Faculty	Other Faculty	Other Patrons
Auxiliary Sciences	6 (3.7%)	68 (8.0%)	74 (3.5%)
World History	16 (9.8)	70 (8.2)	157 (7.5)
European History	44 (27.0)	211 (24.8)	288 (13.7)
British History	11 (6.7)	89 (10.5)	228 (10.9)
History: Asia, Africa, Oceania	14 (8.6)	127 (14.9)	361 (17.2)
General American History	0 (0.0)	26 (3.1)	63 (3.0)
General U.S. History	38 (23.3)	137 (16.1)	520 (24.8)
U.S. Local History	28 (17.2)	88 (10.4)	287 (13.7)
Other American History	6 (3.7)	34 (4.0)	121 (5.8)

Cols. 1 & 2: chi-square=24.72, 8 d.f., p<.01
Cols. 1 & 3: chi-square=35.96, 8 d.f., p<.001

Table 31. Reading Interests in Engineering

Subject	Eng'ing. Faculty	Other Faculty	Other Patrons
General Technology	59 (9.2%)	244 (35.3%)	1,394 (22.5%)
Civil Engr'ing	280 (43.6)	86 (12.4)	1,558 (25.2)
Envir'al Engr'ing	19 (3.0)	61 (8.8)	524 (8.5)
Construction Engr'ing	24 (3.7)	52 (7.5)	357 (5.8)
Mechanical Engr'ing	65 (10.1)	26 (3.8)	416 (6.7)
Electrical Engr'ing	113 (17.6)	67 (9.7)	977 (15.8)
Mining Engr'ing	26 (4.0)	33 (4.8)	168 (2.7)
Chemical Engr'ing	29 (4.5)	73 (10.5)	539 (8.7)
Manufactures	27 (4.2)	50 (7.2)	256 (4.1)

Cols. 1 & 2: chi-square=301.85, 8 d.f., p<.001
Cols. 1 & 3: chi-square=175.33, 8 d.f., p<.001

Table 32. Reading Interests in Foreign Languages

Subject	Foreign Language Faculty	Other Faculty	Other Patrons
Other Languages	1 (1.4%)	41 (14.0%)	96 (19.8%)
Slavic Language and Literature	1 (1.4)	69 (23.5)	65 (13.4)
French Literature	17 (23.0)	78 (26.6)	80 (16.5)
Italian Literature	0 (0.0)	34 (11.6)	34 (7.0)
Spanish and Portuguese Literature	43 (58.1)	37 (12.6)	41 (8.4)
German Literature	12 (16.2)	34 (11.6)	170 (35.0)

Cols. 1 & 2: chi-square= 89.47, 5 d.f., p<.001
Cols. 1 & 3: chi-square=139.77, 5 d.f., p<.001

For four of the six literatures in which the borrowing of departmental faculty could be compared to that of other readers, faculty approach their own literatures in a way which differs rather dramatically from the approach of others. The English department borrows more English literature than American literature, while other faculty have the opposite preference and there is no appreciable difference for nonfaculty borrowers. English faculty read very little unreclassified fiction in English, but this class accounts for over 10 percent of use by external faculty and by all other patrons. The philosophy and religion department's marked preference for materials in philosophy over those in religion (a preference reversed by the other two groups) provides the strongest example of a distinctive reading pattern. Many subfields of engineering are equally popular with all three patron groups, but the engineering faculty show much more interest in materials in civil engineering than the other groups do. Similarly, foreign languages faculty read more in Spanish and Portuguese literature than in all other foreign languages and literatures combined, but other patrons make only modest use of such materials. The departments of sociology and history distribute their reading across their "own" literatures in fairly representative ways. All in all, the data cannot be said to have proved conclusively that academic departments approach their subject literatures in distinctive ways, but they quite strongly support such an argument. Certainly those libraries which contemplate allocating collection development funds might want to consider the chances that their departmental faculty will serve as very imperfect representatives for the reading interests of anyone but themselves.

Chapter 4

Further Explorations of Interdisciplinary Relationships

Circulation data on the reading patterns of faculty from many departments have facilitated comparisons with citation studies of cross-disciplinary use. To the extent that circulation data and citation findings agree about specific relationships among disciplines, greater confidence in the results of either approach will be justified. In the main, the relationships among disciplines which the circulation data describe are consistent with the findings of citation studies. However, a number of specific bibliometric findings, such as the dependence of geologists on physics, are replicated ambiguously or not at all in the circulation data, while the circulation records reveal some strong interests which citation studies do not anticipate. Of course, the records of a few individuals with atypical interests can skew circulation data, especially for small departments. The resulting findings are unrepresentative in their specifics, but they are representative in the sense that they remind librarians that in any community there will be readers who wish to pursue wholly unpredictable and idiosyncratic interests that defy all assumptions.

While the present data replicate many findings from citation studies, they indicate important differences in the extent to which specialized literatures satisfy the needs of most disciplines. Generally, those fields which cite their own literatures most heavily also use a heavy concentration of library materials in their own literatures. The findings for the departments of mathematics and geography are in accord with the citation literature in showing, respectively, a very high and a very low degree of dependence on endogenous literatures. Although the difference between mathematicians' practices and those of geographers is in the same direction whether measured by citation counts or circulation records, in both cases the library data show a greater dependence on external literatures than citation counts reveal. This distinction is typical of most of the comparisons that could be made. The difference between library use within specialized literatures and citation of endogenous materials is found not only within the sciences and social sciences, but within the humanities as well; the circulation data show a wider use of literatures by historians and specialists in literature than was revealed by a citation study conducted for the National Enquiry.[1]

Satariano has argued that most social scientists' use of their personal libraries is more specialized than their citation practices.[2] Comparisons between citation studies and the present data suggest that library use defines the other extreme from the reading of personal libraries and subscriptions and is most catholic of all. This difference is undoubtedly due in part to the fact that most authors use the monographic literature, which circulation data capture, more broadly than the journal literature typically studied in citation analysis, but differences in citing and library behavior appear to be too large to be explicable in these terms alone. The data shown in Table 33, taken from Broadus's review article of citation practices in the social sciences, are fairly typical of the distinction between library use and citation practices with respect to a discipline's use of its own literature. The rank order among the disciplines is identical in citation data and library use, but in each case endogenous materials account for a smaller share of library use.[3]

Table 33. Use of Endogenous Materials by Social Scientists

	Citations	VPI&SU Circ. Data
Economics	68.6%	55.9%
Education	62.1	32.4
Sociology	33.0	31.5
Political Science	30.9	13.1

NOTE: Where Broadus's review covers more than one article on a discipline's practices, the reported percentages of self-citation have been averaged. "Economics" and "Business Administration" are considered endogenous literatures for economists.

Many of the most significant and influential bibliometric studies have focused, not on dependencies among disciplines, but on the characteristics of individual disciplines that their citation practices reveal. It is a common precept in citation studies that both the mean age of citations in a discipline's literature and the proportion of citations to the field itself are reliable measures of its "paradigmatic development," in Thomas Kuhn's sense. Kuhn refers to the paradigm of a science as one of a number of "universally recognized scientific achievements that for a time provide model problems and solutions to a community of practitioners." In a latter elaboration, he indicated a second, broader meaning of the term, in which it "stands for the entire constellation of beliefs, values, techniques, and so on shared by the members of a given community." [4]

It would probably not be an exaggeration to state that Kuhn's perspective has itself provided the main paradigm for the sociology of science. Citation studies typically take a high incidence of references to both recent and endogenous literature as evidence that the fundamental theoretical basis of a discipline has been agreed upon and that neither the major theoretical agenda nor the legitimate paths of discovery and inference are in dispute. This being the case, the field can practice "normal science," extending and refining the paradigm and solving problems whose significance is universally acknowledged by using techniques whose validity all practitioners accept.

Many observers have noted the extent to which the physical and social sciences differ in their practices and have argued that the latter have yet to attain the maturity of the former, with its consensus on the fundamental issues of importance. Arms and Arms have pointed to the "ill-defined literature" of the social sciences, which they relate to overlap among disciplines.[5] Campbell, in the essay in which he gave the term ethnocentrism its first bibliometric application, attributes the same problem to the social sciences, concluding that "the present organization of content into departments is highly arbitrary, a product in large part of historical accident." [6]

In Table 34, each discipline's dependence on its own literature is compared with its use of the remaining literatures of its tradition and with its dependence on the other major traditions. Literatures are grouped into the three large, traditional areas of knowledge. The subject fields "History," "Language and Literature," and "Other Humanities," already one level of aggregation above the original categorization of eighty-one subject literatures, are again grouped, now forming the global area "Humanities." Individual subjects previously grouped under "Economics and Business Administration" or "Social Sciences" are grouped as "All Social Sciences." Subjects from "Physical Sciences," "Life Sciences," and "Technology" are grouped as "Natural Sciences." "Other" literatures remain as before. Circulation statistics for each department in the College of Arts and Sciences with one hundred or more books are displayed, with the exception of biology, the one life science department.

Table 34. Use of Materials in Major Areas by Faculty in Arts and Sciences

Humanities Dept.	Own Lit.	Other Hum.	All Soc. Sci.	Nat. Sci.	Other
Art	46.6%	43.6	4.9	1.2	3.7
English	50.4%	33.2	5.2	6.0	5.2
Foreign Languages	40.7%	45.1	0.5	5.5	8.2
History	28.3%	13.0	32.4	15.3	11.1
Philosophy & Religion	35.2%	25.7	13.0	13.5	12.6

Science Dept.	Own Lit.	Other Nat. Sci.	All Soc. Sci.	Hum.	Other
Chemistry	46.8%	23.5	1.6	22.9	5.2
Geology	48.4%	26.7	5.6	3.2	16.1
Mathematics	68.4%	20.7	2.1	5.0	3.8
Physics	50.3%	31.5	3.4	8.7	6.1
Statistics	34.7%	45.8	7.6	6.3	5.6

Social Science Dept.	Own Lit.	Other Soc. Sci.	Hum.	Nat. Sci.	Other
Geography	7.8%	51.7	25.4	9.1	6.0
Political Science	13.1%	38.2	16.1	5.1	27.6
Psychology	10.5%	28.1	25.4	30.7	5.3
Sociology	37.1%	26.1	23.0	6.6	7.2

NOTE: The definition of each department's own literature is obvious, with the following exceptions: English: English and American Literatures, English Language, Unreclassified Fiction; Foreign Languages: Other Languages, Slavic, French, Italian, German, and Spanish and Portuguese Literatures; Philosophy and Religion: Philosophy and Religion; Mathematics: Mathematics and Statistics; Statistics: Mathematics and Statistics; Sociology: Sociology and Anthropology

Most of the humanities departments and every science department except statistics read their own literatures most heavily, as shown in the left-hand column. This is true for only one social science, sociology, and the remaining social sciences rely considerably more on the other social sciences than on their own literatures. Indeed, for the remaining three social sciences departments, this would be the case even if "Economics" and "Business Administration" were not grouped as social sciences. The very low degree to which the social science departments depend on their own literatures buttresses the conclusions of citation studies with library use data, and also supports Line's argument that "each discipline in the social sciences is much less clearly defined than in the sciences (and) the scatter of potentially relevant information is much greater in the social sciences than in most sciences." [7]

Of course, the opposite of scattering would be a high degree of ethnocentrism, so that a discipline can hardly avoid being characterized by one term of opprobrium or another if value-laden concepts are taken too seriously. If the proper study of the social sciences is man, it should be quite natural for social scientists to find in history and various cultural expressions primary materials for their work. Crane would suggest that the cross-disciplinary reading among the social sciences is evidence of a difference between the paradigms of the social sciences and those of the natural sciences, rather than of the absence of theoretical development in social science. In her view, the paradigms of the social sciences are typically specialized and cannot be cataloged under hierarchical disciplinary lines. [8] Storer takes much the same position: "It may be argued whether the social sciences have yet attained consensus on basic disciplinary paradigms, but it seems reasonable to assume that most specialties within these disciplines have approximated a condition of normal science." [9]

The social sciences also contain a number of theoretical perspectives too broad to match disciplinary lines. As examples of concepts which appear to display the requisite theoretical maturity and coherence but which cross disciplinary boundaries, one might consider the notions of relative deprivation, which is applicable both to small groups and to the explanation of political revolution, and of functionalism, a concept applied by its advocates to social groups as disparate as the Trobriand Islanders and the modern political state. The social scientist interested in developing these theories would see himself as traveling on a single track, but a researcher following his bibliometric trail might consider it proof of a high degree of scattering.

Although the percentage of endogenous use by social scientists is lower than that for the other major traditions of knowledge, it is evidence of a coherence and closure among the literatures which at least partially justifies Garfield's view of the social sciences as a "third culture." [10] Earle and Vickery's finding that social scientists rely on their own materials for 58 percent of their citations also suggests the view that, while the social sciences are less self-contained than the natural sciences in their use of subject literatures, they do comprise a reasonably well-defined cluster of literatures and, by inference, of disciplines. [11]

A remarkable contrast to the social sciences, science stands out as the model of a self-contained group of literatures. "Other" classes have been discarded in calculating data for the data shown in Table 35, except for the subject "General Science," which has been included with the sciences. According to the table, social scientists rely on the social science literature for less than two-thirds of their library materials, after the exclusion of "Other" literatures. Science and technology are highly dependent on their own literatures, especially when departments from these areas are viewed together. If self-reliance is a sign of paradigmatic development, then science has indeed achieved a degree of closure the social sciences have yet to attain.

However, as with nearly every comparison between citation and library use findings, the circulation data show more cross-reading than citation studies have established. Earle and Vickery found that science and technology, taken as a whole, cite their own literatures 97.2 percent of the time.[12] This compares to 84.3 percent use of endogenous library materials (78.8 percent if "Other" classes are included). While all of these percentages are high, Earle and Vickery's data and the circulation findings differ by a factor of five or six in the percentage of external literatures used by scientists. The literature of science and technology may or may not be closed, as Earle and Vickery assert, but the library needs of faculty in science and technology fields clearly go beyond the literatures associated with their disciplines.

Table 35. Overall Reading in Humanities, Social Sciences and Science and Technology

DEPARTMENT

Literature	Hum.	Soc. Sci.	Sci. & Eng.
Humanities	78.8%	24.4%	8.9%
Social Sciences	12.0	64.1	6.7
Sciences and Technology	9.1	11.5	84.3

In addition to allowing a reexamination of the extent to which various disciplines rely on their own literatures, the circulation data permit an examination of those relationships among disciplines that citation analyses have established. For example, the data can be used to examine the relationships among the major fields of science and between science itself and other traditions. The conclusion that faculty in engineering depend on the physical sciences for about one-third of their library materials represents by far the most pronounced conflict between the circulation data and a major citation study. The library data for both the physical and the life sciences and their dependent technologies reverse the relationship that Earle and Vickery posit between science and technology so clearly that it would be hard to attribute the contradiction to simple differences between the British National Bibliography and Library of Congress classifications. It should be noted that Earle and Vickery's conclusions are far from aberrant and represent a common perspective among students of science and technology. Marquis and Allen represent this view well in their paraphrase of R. S. Isensen: "'It would appear that most advances in the technological state of the art are based upon no more recent scientific advances than Ohm's Law or Maxwell's equations.'" Marquis and Allen's data generally support the view that "there is little evidence for direct communications between science and technology," and that the communication which does exist is bilateral. They find that technical areas vary widely in the extent to which they depend on more basic scientific work.[13]

A partial explanation of the differences between Earle and Vickery's work and the present study may lie in Price's view that workers in science and technology differ both in their use of external literatures and in their citation practices. Certainly much citing stems from an obligation to acknowledge others' recent contributions and carefully to disavow credit for them. This motivation is not an issue when authors refer to less recent and more basic understandings, and Price would argue that when engineers and others in technological fields refer to the sciences, it is generally to an older body of work. He also suggests that, for workers in technological subjects, publication is not usually the chief goal but is more of a casual by-product of research, and that publications should be seen as an epiphenomenon of technology.[14] If this explanation applies, we should not expect citation studies and library studies ever to agree on the relationship between science and technology. The important thing to learn will be that citation practices and library use represent different behaviors. Library policies should reflect what we know about the latter. A second lesson this explanation would imply is that students of science and technology should not be misled by the biases inherent in citation studies into underestimating the degree to which progress in technology draws on scientific knowledge.

The data also facilitate a reconsideration of the relationships between the life sciences and the physical sciences, allowing us to determine the utility of this distinction. The circulation records of faculty in agriculture and veterinary medicine show only a modest level of interest in the physical sciences. Agriculture faculty borrowed 8.3 percent of their materials in the physical sciences, mainly chemistry, while the faculty of veterinary medicine had no materials at all from the physical sciences. Data for the biology faculty, the one Arts and Sciences department in the life sciences, also show relatively light use of physical science materials (9.5 percent).

The circulation records for other faculty illuminate the opposite direction of interest, from the physical sciences and technology to the life sciences, and show a similarly modest, though significant, degree of interest. Materials in the life sciences provide 8.7 percent of library materials for faculty in the physical sciences, while the engineering faculty depend on life science materials for only 3.0 percent of their use. Certainly the traffic of interest between the two traditions is slight, compared to the very large dependence of science departments on physical science materials and the heavy reliance of life science disciplines on their own literatures. Chemistry provides a significant linkage, and in general the mutual interest of the two areas is greater than the dependence of either tradition on the social sciences or the humanities. Overall, however, the data suggest a reasonably clean distinction between the life sciences and the physical sciences. While such a distinction would justify the common practice of grouping disciplines under the headings of "life" and "physical" sciences, it would also suggest that generalizations about the literatures needed by the sciences as a whole disguise a great deal of detail. The relative independence of the life sciences, the physical sciences, and technology and the role of chemistry as a link between the biological and physical sciences are both consistent with Brown's 1956 study of citation practices in science.[15]

Correlational Analysis and Conjoint Reading

Whether within a library setting or within the institutional structure of scholarship and science, it clearly is important to identify a structure which makes sense of an otherwise overwhelming chaos of information. Baughman has indicated how intimately collection development and both the physical and intellectual organization of the materials a library acquires must depend on an understanding of the structure of use.[16] Implicit and largely untested models of the structure of academic disciplines already exist, and they permeate discussions of library work and of the sociology of science. The very nomenclature without which it would be impossible to discuss knowledge both reflects and tends to reify shared concepts of structure. Merely to say "the humanities" or "the physical sciences" is to convey an assumption which is imposed and strengthened by the phrase itself. To the extent that they establish "who reads what," the circulation data have added to the picture of interdisciplinary relationships which citation studies have traced and have helped to evaluate the utility of these common labels.

Library classification schemes and most thesauri used in indexing reflect beliefs about the structure of literatures to the extent that they group some literatures more closely together than others. Schemes vary in the degree of hierarchy and rigidity they impose on literatures; for example, the Dewey classification is more insistently deductive than the Library of Congress plan in its decimalized levels of hierarchy and in its more consistent specification of the role of geography and chronology in forming call numbers.

While classification schemes and bibliometric analysis both provide pathways to the internal structure of literatures, they differ radically in their approaches. Classification schemes reflect the inherent nature of literatures. For example, the Library of Congress schedule assigns geology to the class "Q" rather than to class "T" on the premise that geology shares the goals, perspectives, and techniques of the sciences rather than those of technology, and that its literature will reflect these orientations. Psychology is grouped with philosophy rather than with the social sciences because it arose from philosophy, and the now anachronistic placement of this literature within the LC classification serves as a reminder of how accurately classification schemes reflect our maps of the world of knowledge.

Indeed, classification schemes provide maps in more than a metaphorical sense, for they determine the shelving location of materials, and in the process dictate the physical proximity of materials in given subjects. Because geology is assigned to Class "Q" rather than to class "T," materials in this literature will reside closer to materials in chemistry and biology than to materials in mining and metallurgy. It is important to note that a classification scheme's cartography of knowledge is not based on, and makes no reference to, the disciplinary affiliation of borrowers. The Library of Congress scheme reflects an expectation that those patrons who use materials in geology--whoever they may be--will also desire materials in chemistry, and will benefit if these subjects can be shelved together.

The approach taken by classification schemes suggests insights from which bibliometric studies could benefit. It is certainly possible to maintain that there is no inherent structure to literatures apart from the use which is made of them. But even if this behavioristic (or nominalistic) argument is accepted, classification schemes enjoy an enviable independence of changing disciplinary boundaries. It is possible for a classification scheme to reflect the consonance between two literatures even though neither may be represented by an academic discipline, or even if there are such disciplines but the cross-reading between them is limited. The rationale for assigning adjacent classifications would be that readers who seek materials in one literature are expected to seek materials in the other as well.

Co-citation analysis and bibliographic coupling are examples of techniques already in use which are not limited to analyzing relationships from the point of view of specific disciplines. However, Price has argued effectively that, while co-citation analysis is very powerful, it is but one of a potentially large number of techniques to assess the underlying structure of literatures and that other approaches, especially those which address levels of aggregation apart from the individual paper, may be useful:

> (T)he structures and analyses revealed by co-citation techniques are relatively independent of our happening to use citation as a way of linking two or more papers. Textual similarity or other indicators of meaning would do just as well and so would sociological similarities like co-authorship. Furthermore, we should not have to limit our discussion to papers or books, portions of such items would also serve, and so would conglomerates of such items. What seems to be at stake is the existence of particles of knowledge which may range in size from the smallest atom-like units to considerable assemblages, and a set of relationships between these particles.[17]

Correlational analyses of the covariance in use across subject literatures may provide an alternative bibliometric strategy, complementing existing techniques in the manner which Price suggests. Such an approach may be especially valuable for library studies because it does not require extensive patron data. Correlational analysis may be used to indicate how strongly interest in a given pair of literatures is associated or to identify clusters of literatures which share a common readership. A fruitful and exciting culmination of correlational analysis could come from the application of factor analysis or various techniques for multi-dimensional scaling, an ambition which McGrath announced for his data in 1976.[18] Such techniques can be very powerful tools for identifying the underlying structure of vast sets of data. In addition to parsimony, they have the advantage of being able to violate some of the constraints of geometric space, so that it is possible for one of two very closely associated phenomenon also to be close to a third phenomenon, while the second would be relatively distant from the third.

Factor analysis and scaling do have some disadvantages, however, especially in that results are quite sensitive to differences in technique and require great subjectivity in interpretation. Even more fundamentally, scaling techniques require that lower-order relationships be reasonably strong; a matrix of only very low correlations will not support scaling. Even if underlying factors can be identified from such a matrix, they will account for a negligible proportion of variance and will be misleading.

The following analyses use correlational techniques to pursue the structural characteristics of subject literatures as far as the faculty data would appear to permit. Each correlation represents the extent to which use in two subject literatures covaries across patrons. The analysis is restricted to active faculty borrowers. Borrowers who had materials in only the categories "Other" and "Unassociated Records" were disregarded, as these are not meaningful subjects. After this deletion, 1,260 active faculty borrowers remained. Correlational analysis is quite "robust" in the technical sense of the word; that is, findings are not greatly affected even when some of the assumptions which should be met before correlations are used do not pertain.

Correlations are, however, sensitive to extreme values in measured parameters, or "outliers." For this reason, chi-square has been used as a complementary technique. In computing chi-square for the relationship between the use of two subject literatures, data were manipulated to produce one observation for each patron, indicating whether the patron was a current borrower of materials in one field, in the other, in neither, or in both. With only one observation per patron, the assumptions of chi-square are not violated, as they were in Chapter 3. Chi-square provides a measure of how likely readers are to use two literatures together, beyond the chance extent to which there would be conjoint reading even if results were random.

The results of correlational analysis of the circulation data offer little hope for successful scaling and suggest that conventional groupings of subject literatures go only so far to summarize and simplify perceptions of most patrons' needs. Of the thirty-six pairs of literatures within the nine subject literatures of history, only four correlations exceed .20 for faculty patrons. "Non-findings" can be informative, and this one might be interpreted by suggesting that patrons who use historical materials generally take a problem approach, using materials in the history of only one part of the world rather than materials in all aspects of history. However, many other correlations between pairs of ostensibly related subject literatures are quite low and do not reach conventional levels of statistical significance.

The tables in the following pages provide evidence of some clusters of subject literatures within the physical sciences, life sciences, and social sciences which are related, but in each case a significant number of literatures normally thought to be related to those shown failed to achieve significant correlations with literatures within the clusters. Overall, the correlational findings indicate that knowledge of some of the fields in which a patron has borrowed materials would only marginally improve our ability to predict the literatures among which the person's remaining books are distributed.

Though none of the correlations among grouped subjects is high, comparisons among them may cast light on some of the larger issues about the relationships among disciplines. Table 36 gives the Pearson correlation coefficients for each pair of grouped subjects, along with rejection levels for statistical significance.[19] The correlations among levels of use in the grouped literatures "History," "Language and Literature," and "Other Humanities" suggest a coherence among these literatures which justifies referring to them as components of a single tradition, the humanities. Interestingly, the correlations between "History" and both "Language and Literature" and "Other Humanities" are higher than those between "History" and either "Economics and Business Administration" or "Social Sciences." This comparison suggests that, regardless of the materials historians themselves use (certainly a valid index of how they approach their work), those who use historical materials heavily are more likely to borrow extensively in the literatures of the other humanities than in those of the social sciences. The data also show a modest relationship between "Social Sciences" and "Economics and Business Administration."

The correlations among the grouped literatures "Physical Sciences," "Life Sciences," and "Technology" are all low, while with one exception the correlations between any of these and other grouped fields are for all practical purposes zero. These findings accord quite well with previous observations that the sciences as a whole tend to be a self-contained literature and that the physical sciences and the life sciences are quite distinct. The relationship between the physical sciences and technology is the highest of the correlations among the three grouped literatures, which might have been predicted from the data on cross-disciplinary reading, but at .154 even this relationship is not strong.

Table 36. Correlations among Use Measures for Grouped Subjects

Hist.							
Lang. & Lit.	.258#						
Other Hum.	.307#	.270#					
Econ. & B.A.	.089*	-.027	-.015				
Social Sci.	.197#	.046	.168#	.248#			
Phys. Sci.	-.016	-.049	.005	-.027	-.038		
Life Sci.	-.007	-.043	-.020	-.036	-.023	.076*	
Tech.	.021	-.046	-.007	.145#	-.031	.154#	.004	
	Hist	Lang& Lit	Other Hum	Econ& B.A.	Soc Sci	Phys Sci	Life Sci	Tech

NOTE: N = 1,260
* Significant at .01.
# Significant at .001

Findings in Table 37 express the relationships among the grouped subjects in terms of chi-square rather than of correlations. Higher values of chi-square represent greater deviations from the extent of conjoint reading between subjects than would be expected on the basis of chance, while small values indicate that the observed number of patrons with books out in two subjects is about what would be expected in the absence of an actual, non-random relationship. Chi-square values are always positive, so that they will be large even when there is significantly *less* conjoint reading than we would expect. For this reason, an asterisk is used to designate those cases in which there are fewer readers of the two literatures under consideration than would be expected.

Generally, the results of the chi-square tests are consistent with the correlational data. Specifically, they support the conclusion that use of materials in history, language and literature, and other humanities literatures is closely related and that use in the social sciences and in economics and business administration covaries significantly. They also substantiate the independence of the science literatures from other literatures. Interestingly, the number of co-readers of materials in the physical and life sciences is almost exactly the number which would be expected on the basis of chance, making the chi-square value close to zero. This finding further demonstrates the independence between these two literatures.

Table 37. Relations among Use in Grouped Literatures: Chi-square Values

	Hist.	Lang. & Lit.	Other Hum.	Econ. B.A.	Soc. Sci.	Phys. Sci.	Life Sci.	Tech.
Hist.								
Lang. & Lit.	71.0							
Other Hum.	82.0	76.8						
Econ. & B. A.	20.6	0.3	0.8					
Soc. Sci.	38.9	9.8	38.5	90.2				
Phys. Sci.	11.4*	21.9*	7.2*	7.0*	19.1*			
Life Sci.	0.5*	9.3*	0.4*	3.0*	3.6*	0.2*		
Tech.	3.5*	11.6*	0.0	2.3	4.5*	36.1	3.6*	

NOTE: * indicates negative relationship.
$p < .05$ at chi-square = 3.9
$p < .01$ at chi-square = 6.7
$p < .001$ at chi-square = 10.9

Close inspection of the correlational data (an 87-by-87 matrix after the inclusion of grouped subjects and the deletion of the subjects "Other" and "Unassociated Records") revealed high correlations for a number of pairs of individual disciplines, but this would be expected as a chance phenonemon with so many observations. To avoid such misleading, freak occurrences, the analysis focused on clusters of individual literatures which shared moderately high inter-subject correlations. Even so, the results of such a *post hoc* inspection of correlations should ideally be replicated by different data before they are accepted. Correlations among all the groups reported here were repeated for graduate student data and were uniformly lower. This difference may indicate greater independence among graduate student use of various literatures due to specialization, which would be consistent with the finding that graduate students are more ethnocentric in their reading. However, it could also indicate that the significant relationships which have been identified are higher than would normally be found.

The correlations and chi-square data revealed several reasonably coherent groups of individual subject literatures. Within the physical sciences, use in the three fundamental literatures of "Mathematics and Statistics," "Physics," and "Chemistry" covaries significantly, as reported in Tables 38 and 39. The relationship between use of materials in mathematics and chemistry, as measured by both correlations and chi-square, is the weakest in the group, which is consistent with findings on these departments' reading. It should be remembered that the data base for correlational analysis and for the analysis of cross-disciplinary reading is the same, so that the correlational results do not represent independent replication of the results on cross-disciplinary use. On the other hand, all faculty readers are included in these data, not just members of the appropriate departments, and the measures are very different, so that findings need not necesarily be confirmed.

Table 38. Correlations among Key Physical Science Literatures

Math. & Stat.			
Physics	.429		
Chemistry	.199	.256	
	Math	Physics	Chem.

NOTE: p<.001 for all relationships.

Table 39. Relationships among Science Literatures: Chi-square

Math. & Stat.			
Physics	63.5		
Chemistry	0.7	65.5	
	Math & Stat.	Physics	Chemistry

NOTE: p<.05 at chi-square = 3.9
p<.01 at chi-square = 6.7
p<.001 at chi-square = 10.9

Within the life sciences, faculty use of five literatures covaries significantly. Tables 40 and 41 report the relationships among use in these literatures. The data on cross-discipinary reading showed that "General Biology" is a common resource for nearly all disciplines in the life sciences, whether they emphasize basic research or applied work with plants or animals. The remainder of the subjects in the cluster pertain to physiology, medicine, and the interface between them.

Table 40. Correlations among Life Science Literatures

Gen. Biol.

	Gen. Biol.	Anat. & Phys.	Micro.	Med.	Vet. Med.
Anat. & Phys.	.267#				
Micro.	.423#	.402#			
Med.	.306#	.321#	.093#		
Vet. Med.	.009	.327#	.139#	.346#	

NOTE: * Significant at .01.
Significant at .001.

Table 41. Relationships among Life Sciences: Chi-square

Gen. Biol.

	Gen. Biol.	Anat. & Phys.	Micro.	Med.	Vet. Med.
Anat. & Phys.	85.0				
Micro.	119.4	43.3			
Med.	21.1	117.4	5.8		
Vet. Med.	6.5	74.7	N/A	69.3	

NOTE: $p<.05$ at chi-square = 3.9
$p<.01$ at chi-square = 6.7
$p<.001$ at chi-square = 10.9
The expected number of conjoint readers of Veterinary Medicine and Microbiology is too low to permit the reliable computation of chi-square.

For all of the small clusters of individual subjects which are shown, a number of subject literatures which might have been expected to covary with the literatures being displayed failed to do so significantly. For example, reading in "Astronomy" and "Geology" does not covary significantly with use of materials in the physical sciences shown, and the use of materials in "Zoology," "Botany," and various fields of agriculture does not covary with use in the life sciences included in the table. An especially large number of possible pairings do not correlate significantly within the social sciences. Use of materials in "Psychology" and in "Education" is related, but the correlations between "Psychology," "Geography," "Anthropology," and "Education" and the literatures shown in Tables 42 and 43 are uniformly low and generally fall short of significance at even the .05 level. These low correlations may cast further doubt on the coherence of the component fields of the social sciences. The social science literatures which do form a cluster generally emphasize the macro-level analysis of modern societies.

Table 42. Correlations among Social Science Literatures

Econ.

	Econ.	Soc.	Poli. Sci.
Soc.	.219		
Poli. Sci.	.263	.258	

NOTE: $p<.001$ for all relationships.

Table 43. Relationships among Social Sciences: Chi-square

Econ.			
Soc.	90.2		
Poli. Sci.	126.8	96.3	
	Econ.	Soc.	Poli. Sci.

NOTE: p<.05 at chi-square = 3.9
p<.01 at chi-square = 6.7
p<.001 at chi-square = 10.9

In general, the statistical measures of the strength of relationships among use in various subjects complement the data on use according to discipline by specifying more accurately the relationships of such literature groups as history or the physical sciences to other traditions. The most significant findings from the point of view of library policy are those which show the relative independence of the scientific literatures from other traditions, the covariance between use in history and other literatures of the humanities, and the relationship between use in the social sciences, economics, and business administration. These findings complement the data on cross-disciplinary use in suggesting logical groupings for collections and services. The findings are reassuring to the extent that they show predictable constellations of literature use for certain fields within the physical sciences, the life sciences, and, to a lesser degree, the social sciences. On the other hand, the present data do not appear to support extensive work in discovering the underlying structure of literature use. Perhaps data from another setting, using different definitions of subjects, could achieve this result. The potential rewards of such work are great, and they commend for this task a high place in the agenda of library research.

Chapter 5

Student Use Of
Subject Literatures

In any study of how a university library is used, a major emphasis on the reading preferences of faculty is appropriate because of their unique contribution to the research mission of higher education. Faculty reading is of particular interest in the present study because it provides the best source of data to illuminate and extend the landscape of interdisciplinary relationships that citation studies have sketched. However, only about one-quarter of the books in circulation at the time of the study were charged to members of the faculty. Nearly 70 percent of books in circulation were charged to students. Graduate students had only slightly more books than undergraduates (36.2 percent of books in circulation versus 33.0 percent), though on a per capita basis graduate students accounted for nearly five times as much circulation activity as did undergraduates.

For the purpose of understanding why book stock is used as it is, then, student records are most valuable. Student use is analyzed in this chapter, but in less detail than was devoted to faculty reading. Further information is available in Appendix B, which provides circulation data for every student program in which students had one hundred books or more. As with the faculty data presented in Chapter 3, data in the appendix are presented in terms of grouped subjects, but reading percentages in those subjects of greatest interest to a college are presented individually.

The most striking characteristic of the student circulation data is the extent to which the reading patterns of graduate students in various fields resemble those of the faculty. This is especially true when aggregated data are considered, but the similarity applies to many specific comparisons as well. Undergraduates in all areas of study rely less on specialized materials than do faculty and graduate students; that is, knowledge of an undergraduate's major gives us significantly less ability to predict what library materials he or she will borrow than we gain from knowing the affiliation of a faculty or graduate student borrower. It should be noted that at VPI&SU, nearly all undergraduates have formal majors throughout their careers. Study in major fields intensifies after the sophomore year, but majors are declared immediately and work in the field of concentration tends to begin early. At an institution where majors are not declared until the junior year, undergraduate use might vary more consistently with field of study.

Table 44 displays the subject distribution of books charged to faculty, graduate students, and undergraduates from each college. Subjects are grouped into the broad areas of "Humanities," "Social Sciences" (including "Economics and Business Administration"), and "Natural Sciences," as before. Generally, the percentage of circulating books in the major area of interest is very similar for faculty and graduate students of the various colleges. Where there are appreciable differences, as in the use of social science literatures by faculty and graduate students in business, education, and the social science disciplines, graduate students depend somewhat more heavily on the broad area of interest than do faculty. The intensive process of socialization to which graduate students are exposed and the effort to make them competent in specialized research skills may account for these differences. Undergraduate use of the major literatures does vary with program of study, but much less so than is true for graduate students.

The distinctions among faculty, graduate student, and undergraduate use of subject literatures are also evident when more specific reading preferences are studied. Table 45 shows the extent to which faculty, graduate students, and undergraduates in various fields use endogenous materials. The table is restricted to those departments in the College of Arts and Sciences with an appreciable number of patrons in each category. Graduate students and faculty use their own literatures very similarly in the sciences, but in the humanities and social sciences, graduate students read more narrowly. In most cases, undergraduates rely on the literatures associated with their major fields for less of their reading than do the other patron groups. In the physical sciences especially, undergraduate majors depend much less heavily on materials in their own disciplines than do faculty and graduate students.

Table 44. Faculty and Student Reading in Major Subject Areas

College	Group	All Hum.	All Soc. Sci.	Nat. Sci.	Other
Agriculture	Fac.	7.6%	14.7	69.7	8.0
	Grad.	4.3%	16.4	70.3	9.0
	Und.	15.7%	17.3	55.7	11.3
Architecture	Fac.	21.8%	34.5	11.1	32.6
	Grad.	21.5%	31.8	17.2	29.5
	Und.	27.4%	9.3	29.0	34.3
Business	Fac.	13.3%	64.3	11.4	11.0
	Grad.	7.6%	73.4	9.9	9.2
	Und.	28.3%	42.5	18.8	10.4
Education	Fac.	19.4%	52.2	19.2	9.3
	Grad.	7.8%	70.2	10.1	11.9
	Und.	16.1%	30.1	28.4	25.4
Engineering	Fac.	6.9%	9.8	75.8	7.5
	Grad.	4.0%	10.6	77.9	7.5
	Und.	17.0%	18.8	54.8	9.4
Home	Fac.	11.0%	30.1	53.4	5.5
Economics	Grad.	8.5%	46.4	36.7	8.4
	Und.	16.2%	31.5	42.5	9.9
Humanities	Fac.	74.2%	11.3	7.3	7.3
	Grad.	73.8%	10.1	5.1	11.1
	Und.	48.7%	24.6	15.7	11.1
Sciences	Fac.	9.5%	3.6	79.8	7.1
	Grad.	5.4%	5.0	79.9	9.7
	Und.	29.1%	14.1	45.3	11.5
Social	Fac.	21.2%	55.6	8.9	14.3
Sciences	Grad.	11.7%	64.5	17.4	6.4
	Und.	27.6%	52.8	12.1	7.5
Veterinary	Fac.	10.4%	0.4	87.1	2.0
Medicine	Grad.	20.0%	12.0	65.0	3.0
	Und.	N/A	N/A	N/A	N/A

The breadth of undergraduate reading can also be assessed by examining the number of patrons in various fields with books out in each major area. There are seventy-two combinations of the eight broad subjects ("History," "Language and Literature," etc.) and the colleges or areas of the College of Arts and Sciences. For sixty-three of these seventy-two intersections of broad subjects and fields of study, at least twenty-five undergraduates from the designated college had books charged out in the designated subject. There are no "empty cells" for either graduate students or undergraduates in such a matrix. In other

Table 45. Faculty and Student Reading in Specialized Literatures

	Faculty	Graduate	Under-graduate
English	50.4%	67.5%	50.1%
History	28.3%	50.3%	45.8%
Geography	7.8%	19.4%	15.7%
Political Science	13.1%	33.0%	8.7%
Psychology	10.5%	29.0%	10.7%
Sociology	37.1%	38.4%	38.0%
Chemistry	46.8%	50.9%	17.9%
Geology	48.4%	50.1%	20.6%
Mathematics	68.4%	67.0%	17.5%
Physics	50.3%	57.5%	9.9%
Statistics	34.7%	60.4%	26.7%

NOTE: For sociology, "Sociology" and "Anthropology" are considered endogenous literatures. For English, the literatures "English Language," "English Literature," "American Literature," and "Unreclassified fiction" are considered endogenous. The subject literature "Mathematics and Statistics" is considered endogenous for patrons in both of those departments.

words, at least one graduate student and at least one undergraduate from each college had books charged out in each broad subject field at the time of the survey.

Student Reading and Subject Relationships

In some fields it would require only a small exaggeration to state that faculty and graduate students use subject literatures identically. The similarity is especially pronounced for reading within the College of Engineering. Table 46 displays faculty and graduate student use of library materials in engineering and documents the extent of this similarity of interest. The table reports reading by faculty and graduate students in engineering for all instances where a specific literature accounted for over 10 percent of faculty reading and where both faculty and graduate students in a given department had one hundred or more books in use.

Insofar as faculty and graduate students use subject literatures similarly, the circulation records of the students replicate some of the major conclusions about interdisciplinary relationships which were based on faculty circulation records. In drawing conclusions about the relationships among disciplines from the circulation statistics of graduate students, it should still be borne in mind that graduate students are not full-fledged professional researchers and that their reading is somewhat constrained by the curriculum. Obviously, undergraduate reading patterns will be least valuable in tracing inherent relationships among disciplines.

Table 46. Major Interests of Faculty and Graduate Students in Engineering

Department	Literature	Faculty Percent	Graduate Student Percent
Civil Engr.	Bus. Admin.	10.5	7.4
Civil Engr.	Civil Engr.	31.8	35.3
ESM	Math. and Stat.	34.5	40.5
ESM	Physics	15.1	5.6
ESM	Civil Engr.	18.3	30.7
Electrical Engr.	Math. and Stat.	18.3	20.6
Electrical Engr.	Electrical Engr.	35.8	37.9
IEOR	Economics	18.5	15.7
IEOR	Math. and Stat.	22.3	23.5
IEOR	Manufactures	15.5	7.6
Mechanical Engr.	Physics	10.6	5.7
Mechanical Engr.	Civil Engr.	15.8	19.2
Mechanical Engr.	Mechanical Engr.	11.2	11.0

NOTE: ESM represents the Department of Engineering Science and Mechanics. IEOR represents the Department of Industrial Engineering and Operations Research.

The circulation records of graduate students bear out Narin's unidirectional "natural sequence" of interest among science subjects even more strongly than do the faculty records. Figure 4 illustrates the degree to which graduate student records substantiate the sequence of asymmetrical dependencies among biochemistry, chemistry, physics, and mathematics. The flow of interest among fields in this sequence is more nearly unidirectional for graduate student reading than for faculty reading, especially in that graduate students in mathematics do not show as much interest in the physics literature as is shown by the mathematics faculty. In the figure, names stand for both departments and literatures, as they did in Chapter 3. However, since biochemistry was not defined as a subject literature, the chemistry department's use of materials in all the life sciences is shown. Graduate students in each of the departments shown have well over one hundred books except for the Department of Biochemistry and Nutrition, where graduate students had only thirty-three books in circulation. Arrows represent reading by a department in a subject literature. The significant degree to which the top percentages in the figure exceed the bottom percentages supports Narin's argument, as was the case with faculty reading.[1]

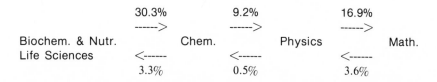

Figure 4:   Sequence of Dependencies for Graduate Students

Graduate student records also replicate the faculty records in demonstrating a generally one-sided relationship between the sciences and technology. This relationship is most markedly asymmetrical for faculty and approaches parity for undergraduates, as indicated by Figures 5, 6, and 7 (from which the biology department and its various offerings have not been excluded). The graduate student records closely resemble those of the faculty and add significant weight to the argument that, whatever their citation practices might indicate, engineers rely heavily on the literature of the physical sciences. Graduate students in engineering make particulary heavy use of materials in "Mathematics and Statistics" (20.9 percent of their use), which is also the physical science literature most heavily used by engineering faculty. This one subject accounts for 40.5 percent of use by graduate students in engineering science and mechanics.

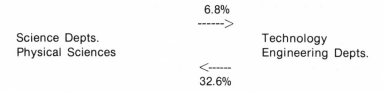

Figure 5:   Sciences and Technology: Faculty

Figure 6:   Physical Sciences and Technology: Graduate Students

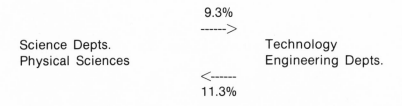

Figure 7: Physical Sciences and Technology: Undergraduates

The graduate student data can also be used to extend and refine arguments about the relationships between life sciences and their dependent technologies. Graduate students in agriculture make significant use of those life science literatures considered "basic" ("General Biology" through "Microbiology" in the subject list). Like their faculty mentors, graduate students in agriculture use the basic life science literatures more than applied life science literatures ("Medicine" through "Wildlife and Fisheries"), though the preference is not nearly so strong. "General Biology," "Botany," and "Anatomy and Physiology" each account for between 6 and 7 percent of charges to graduate students in agriculture. Table 47 shows how both faculty and graduate students in the College of Agriculture distribute their interests across these broad literatures.

Table 47. Life Sciences Use by Faculty and Graduate Students in Agriculture

Literature	Faculty	Graduate Students
Basic Life Sciences	34.2%	24.6%
Applied Life Sciences	18.4	22.8

Graduate student records are especially valuable for examining the relationship between basic and applied life sciences because, whereas there is only one faculty department, biology, in the pure life sciences, graduate programs are offered in botany, microbiology, and zoology. The records for faculty in the biology department showed a very strong preference for materials in basic life sciences and only modest interest in agriculture, medicine, and other applied life sciences. Graduate students in botany, microbiology, and zoology show a similar preference, as indicated in Table 48. "General Biology" is a particularly useful literature to these disciplines, providing 16.9 percent of materials to graduate students in botany, 25.9 percent for students in microbiology, and 20.3 percent of use for graduate students in zoology. All in all, the graduate student data replicate faculty circulation records in showing that disciplines in the applied life sciences depend heavily on materials in basic life sciences, but that, as with the relationship between the physical sciences and technology, this level of interest is only weakly reciprocated.

Table 48. Life Sciences Read by Graduate Students in Basic Life Sciences

DEPARTMENT

Literature	Botany	Microbiol.	Zoology
Basic Life Sciences	65.2%	65.7%	50.2%
Applied Life Sciences	11.2	10.2	9.7

Student records also tend to parallel faculty data in substantiating the relative independence of the physical sciences and technology, on the one hand, and the life sciences and their applied disciplines, on the other. Graduate students in the physical science disciplines and in engineering rely on the life sciences for only 3.3 percent and 3.8 percent of their materials, respectively. Graduate students in agriculture do use the physical sciences for 11.3 percent of their materials (4.4 percent in chemistry), but only one of the one hundred books charged to graduate students in veterinary medicine was in a physical science. Similarly, graduate students in the life sciences proper make relatively light use of physical science materials, which provided 6.5 percent of use by graduate students in both microbiology and zoology, but which were not in use at all by graduate students in botany.

Undergraduate records also show a modest interdependence between the physical sciences and the life sciences. Life science materials accounted for 7.7 percent of circulations to undergraduates in the physical sciences and for 6.1 percent of circulations to engineering undergraduates. Materials in the physical sciences were significantly used by undergraduates in biochemistry, providing 17.2 percent of their materials, but accounted for only 2.9 percent of biology majors' use and 3.1 percent of the books charged to undergraduates in agriculture. Like the faculty data, the circulation records of students indicate that the traditions of the physical and life sciences are reasonably independent and that the distinction between them is a productive one. By the same token, they indicate that, apart from the statement that the sciences are relatively self-contained in their use of subject literatures, generalizations about the literatures of use to the sciences as a whole may sacrifice a great deal of precision for little gain.

Graduate student records also replicate faculty records in demonstrating that psychologists depend on the literature of the life sciences for much of their library use. The life sciences account for 32.6 percent of circulations to graduate students in psychology, whereas social sciences other than psychology account for only 15.7 percent of use. Undergraduate psychology majors, however, read more in the other social sciences (36.6 percent) than in the life sciences (13.0 percent). The latter finding is consistent with McGrath's data from the University of Southwestern Louisiana. However, McGrath found that graduate students in psychology prefer the social science literatures to the life sciences, a preference which is reversed in the VPI&SU data.[2] In general, the circulation records of students in the social sciences confirm the conclusion that there is much cross-reading among the social sciences, with sociology and economics having an especially wide appeal, and that patrons from social science disciplines also depend quite heavily on materials entirely outside of the social sciences. About 20 percent of charges to graduate students in both political science and sociology were in "Economics," while data for graduate and undergraduate students in all social science fields show that each group used "Sociology" for nearly 20 percent of its materials. Just over half (51.5 percent) of the materials used by graduate students were outside the grouped subject "Social Sciences," while for undergraduates the comparable figure was just under two-thirds (64.3 percent).

Faculty circulation records provided the basis for arguments about the place of history as a discipline. The faculty data showed that members of the history department rely significantly more on the literatures of the social sciences, especially if economics and business administration are included, than on language and literature or other humanities. The circulation records of history graduate students show the same preference, with a somewhat larger degree of difference. History graduate students rely on the social sciences for 15.6 percent of their materials, or 21.5 percent if economics and business administration are included, but humanities literatures besides history account for only 5.6 percent of their books. Undergraduate history majors, however, have a slight preference for the literatures of the other humanities, which comprise 19.2 percent of their books compared to 13.3 percent in the social sciences and 16.7 percent if economics and business administration are included. Interestingly, McGrath's data also show that history graduate students read more in the social sciences than in the humanities, but that undergraduates use more materials in the humanities.[3]

Explaining Large Differences in Literature Use

The circulation data show that faculty and graduate students read quite heavily in their own fields, even though they use library materials much more broadly than citation studies would lead us to expect. Because these groups use materials in their own literatures so intensively, the overall use of subject literatures is very much a function of the population of users from each major field. The disciplines in which the ratio of active graduate student borrowers to active faculty borrowers is highest are the colleges of education, architecture, home economics, and engineering. Not surprisingly, the overall percentage of graduate circulation exceeds the overall percentage of faculty circulation in the subjects "Education," "Architecture," "Home Economics," and the grouped subject "Technology." Campus demographics significantly account for differences in the overall reading preferences of the various patron classs, a possibility which was raised in the initial discussion of use according to patron class.

That demographics should play such a large role is not surprising, and the point is somewhat obvious. Yet very little attention has been paid to the extent to which differences in the makeup of university communities may account for the rather significant differences in literature use which surface whenever book use at two or more institutions is compared. If use is as dependent on the makeup of patron populations as the data suggest, and if in turn campus populations vary widely, literatures which are heavily used at one institution may be in much less demand at another.

Chapter 2 concluded with a discussion of various differences among the reading preferences of the five patron classes. While a number of specific hypotheses were advanced to account for some of the ways in which faculty, students, and other patron groups approach subject literatures, it quickly became apparent that further progress could not be made except by reference to the literatures used by faculty and students in given disciplines. Subsequent analyses have provided two methods of explaining differences in overall use patterns. By focusing on the number of potential borrowers in various fields, demographic analysis accounts for use in terms of the relative mix of populations with specific interests. Analyses of how users in given fields do, in fact, approach subject literatures make it possible to account for literature use in terms of the differential appeal of subject literatures to specific patron groups. The two approaches are especially powerful when they can be combined, which occurs whenever the data show that patrons from a given discipline are numerous and also have highly focused interests.

Both of these techniques are useful in explaining some of the broadest differences among use by faculty, graduate students, and undergraduates. In Table 49, these differences are presented in very general terms. Subjects are grouped into the global categories of "Humanities," "Social Sciences," and "Natural Sciences" (including "Technology").

Table 49. Faculty and Student Use of Broad Subject Literatures

Literature	Faculty	Graduate	Under-graduate
Humanities	29.6%	11.4%	26.1%
Social Sciences	23.1	33.1	26.2
Natural Sciences	36.5	44.7	34.9
Other	10.9	10.8	12.8

The table shows a number of significant differences in the library materials used by the three patron groups and invites an explanation of how these differences come about. Demographic arguments have been advanced to account for the fact that graduate students use materials in the social and natural sciences more intensively than faculty do, by attributing the difference to the larger proportion of graduate students than of faculty in the colleges of education, engineering, and home economics. The argument could equally well have been made by showing how relatively low is the proportion of graduate students to faculty in the humanities.

There are other pronounced differences in the literatures used by faculty, graduate students, and undergraduates. Graduate students use the literatures of the sciences and the social sciences more intensively than undergraduates, while undergraduates make much more use of materials in the humanities than is made by graduate students. The explanation for graduate students' heavier use of materials in the social sciences appears to be partly demographic, but mainly to stem from the highly focused literature needs of graduate students in certain fields. Graduate students in the College of Education account for much of the use of the social science literature by graduate students. In fact, they account for 32.7 percent of graduate student use of these literatures, whereas graduate students in the social sciences account for only 14.3 percent. Education students comprise 10.5 percent of active graduate student borrowers, but only 5.1 percent of undergraduates with books in use. Graduate students in education also are much more narrowly interested in the social science literatures than are education undergraduates; the social sciences provided 60.6 percent of the materials of interest to the graduate students, but only 22.7 percent of use by the undergraduates. While graduate students are generally more ethnocentric in the use of library materials, the difference is not usually this large. The graduate students' greater use of social science materials, including those in "Education," appears then to stem both from differences in population makeup and from differences in preferred literatures.

The relative use by graduate students and undergraduates of materials in the natural sciences and technology and in the humanities varies greatly. Demographic analysis provides a partial explanation for this difference, since 12.6 percent of active undergraduate borrowers, but only 2.8 percent of active graduate student borrowers, are in humanities programs. However, demographic explanations do not explain all of these differences in use. General requirements for undergraduate education appear to explain an additional, small part of the difference. Undergraduates in engineering and the sciences rely on materials in the humanities for 21.1 percent of their use, while undergraduates in the humanities use materials in science and technology for 15.7 percent of their library materials. The comparable patterns of cross-disciplinary reading for graduate students are much lower, and the exchange is essentially even (about 5 percent in each direction). General undergraduate requirements appear then to require that students in scientific and technological areas use basic materials in the humanities somewhat more than they require humanities students to use materials in the sciences.

The reading interests of undergraduates in engineering provide an additional explanation for the lower use of science materials by undergraduates. Undergraduates in engineering are nearly as dependent as faculty and graduate students on the engineering literatures grouped under "Technology," but they make much less use of materials in the physical sciences. Undergraduates use fewer materials in mathematics and statistics, in particular, than do faculty and graduate students in engineering. Whether undergraduates in engineering are primarily exposed to their discipline as a system of techniques or whether their grounding in basic physical sciences is achieved through textbook education, the data cannot indicate. Clearly, though, the relationship between engineering and basic sciences is more salient for the work of engineering faculty than for students. As an example, faculty in chemical engineering use chemistry for 40.6 percent of their library materials, while graduate students in this field use the chemical literature for 19.4 percent of their materials and undergraduates rely on materials in chemistry for only 8.4 percent of their use. Table 50 shows the distribution of materials in several basic sciences and in technology to faculty, graduate students, and undergraduates in engineering.

Table 50. Use of Selected Materials by Patrons in Engineering

Subject	Faculty	Graduate	Under-graduate
Mathematics and Statistics	16.3%	20.9%	3.8%
Physics	9.0	4.2	3.2
Chemistry	4.3	2.4	1.4
Technology	40.2	43.1	37.5

General Conclusions and Some Limitations on Generalizing

Because the approach taken here so closely resembles McGrath's, it is possible to make much more general comparisons with his results and to begin to have some confidence in conclusions which both studies support. McGrath's data show that graduate students are much more ethnocentric in their reading than undergraduates. He found that graduate students in twelve of eighteen departments relied on their own subject literatures for at least one-third of their library materials, but that undergraduates in only four of forty-three majors depended so heavily on specialized literatures. Certainly the circulation data from the present study support the same conclusion.

Largely because undergraduate "insiders" make less intensive use of their own literatures, McGrath also found that most literatures are more supportive when undergraduate reading is considered than when graduate student records are examined. In other words, a larger percentage of undergraduate subject reading is typically by outsiders. For fourteen of the eighteen literatures in which the comparison could be made, McGrath found literatures to be more supportive for undergraduate use. In general, the present data replicate this conclusion. At a greater level of detail, the present results do not match McGrath's so consistently, though it is hardly surprising that highly detailed findings should differ more than do more general statements. In addition, the supportiveness scores for the various literatures from the present analysis show no similarity to McGrath's, a difference which is not surprising since supportiveness scores depend heavily on the makeup of user populations.[4]

Despite the caution which should be exercised in interpreting highly detailed data, circulation data do provide a measure of discrimination and detail which it would be foolish to overlook. The details of circulation records are especially useful in revealing the interests of interstitial disciplines not easily approached by citation studies and in reconsidering stereotypes and broad generalizations about the interests of given disciplines. Most campuses support a variety of interdisciplinary programs, yet the library literature rarely treats the needs of patrons in these fields. For example, bibliometricians have apparently ignored the interests of researchers in public administration, which has not attained the status of many older disciplines and which is not represented on many campuses. At VPI&SU, graduate students and undergraduates in public administration make significant use of materials in political science and sociology. Economics and business administration make up 30 percent of graduate student use and 47.7 percent of undergraduate use for students in this program. By their nature, most explicitly interdisciplinary programs will draw on disparate literatures in this manner. It is important not to ignore the library needs of patrons in these fields, but mental images of higher education which reflect traditional lines of disciplines and colleges make such omissions all too easy to commit.

Similarly, facile mental images about faculty and students in major colleges can lead to distorted impressions of library needs. From a distance it is easy to generalize about the library needs of such colleges as architecture, education, or home economics. Yet the circulation records of graduate students in these colleges show that specific programs vary widely in their orientations. The circulation records of graduate students in education provide an apt example. Graduate students in junior and community college education and in educational administration rely on the subject "Education" for over 50 percent of their reading. This subject is of little interest to graduate students in physical education, who rely on the life sciences for 31.3 percent of their reading and on "Recreation" for 34.1 percent.

Circulation records for faculty in architecture and home economics revealed a broad distribution of interest across major fields. Yet a closer look at disaggregated data showed that departments within these colleges use highly specialized and dissimilar library materials. Student records for departments within architecture and home economics show the same differences in use as were found for the faculty in these areas. Undergraduates in the architecture program within the College of Architecture rely on "Architecture" for 31.6 percent of their materials and on various humanities fields for 33.8 percent. But students in building construction, another major offered by the college, use materials in these fields for less than 8 percent of their reading and rely on the various literature of "Technology" for 45.8 percent of their use. Graduate students with an architecture concentration use materials in "Architecture" (30.7 percent) and the humanities (31.6 percent) heavily. But the graduate offerings of the college also include programs in urban affairs and in urban and regional planning; students in these two programs use the literature of the social sciences, including economics and business administration, for 73.0 percent and 64.6 percent of their materials, respectively. Any summary which reported only the aggregated reading interests of students in the College of Architecture would present a distorted image of reality. No program within architecture approaches literatures in the omniverous, almost dilettantish manner that such a report would indicate.

Faculty circulation records for the departments within home economics showed that faculty in the Department of Human Nutrition and Foods (HNF) used life science materials extensively, while those in the Department of Management, Housing, and Family Development (MHFD) found the social sciences more useful to their work. Student records, shown in Table 51, reflect the same distinctions. Again, to report only the overall reading patterns of students in these colleges would be to distort reality in much the same way that one misleads by reporting only average measures of height, income, or intelligence for highly dissimilar individuals in a group. At least within fields which embrace a range of interests, the department, and not the college, would appear to be the most useful unit of analysis if reading patterns are to be described with precision.

Table 51. Reading by Students in HNF and MHFD

Dept.	GRADUATE			UNDERGRADUATE		
	All Soc. Sci.	All Nat. Sci.	Number of Books	All Soc. Sci.	All Nat. Sci.	Number of Books
Human Nutrition and Foods	20.0%	65.3%	265	15.7%	69.2%	351
Management, Housing and Family development	65.3%	20.7%	473	49.5%	25.1%	275

The library needs of students do not always weigh heavily in library planning decisions, partly for political reasons and partly because students are a less well understood group. Arguments for integrated rather than compartmentalized services were based on faculty reading patterns, which are significantly more eclectic than citation studies would imply. While graduate students appear to read somewhat more narrowly than faculty, undergraduates read in a much less predictable and selective fashion. Certainly this finding supports the same arguments for a holistic approach to library services. Students do not normally cite and we know nothing about their personal libraries and subscriptions, but it is almost certainly true that for students, no less than for faculty, a library system provides the single best form of access to literatures across the entire span of knowledge.

Chapter 6

Use and the Structure of Library Systems

If systems of academic libraries are viewed in very general terms, there are few characteristics which vary so widely from one system to another as the degree to which services are centralized. While Harvard has over one hundred libraries, many of which are autonomous or semiautonomous, other library systems share a single authority and have discouraged, if not officially banned, branch libraries. Both the costs and the benefits of separate library units are great. The choices which colleges and universities make about library structure reflect professional judgments about the relative advantages or disadvantages of centralized services as well as powerful political forces within most academic communities. Branch libraries can be enormously convenient to their clientele, especially those whose work is highly specialized or who need to consult reference materials frequently while working with laboratory or other apparatus physically remote from the main library. Indeed, Dougherty and Blomquist have found that use of a library facility varies significantly with its proximity to a patron, even when the entire range of distances under comparison is restricted to the distances between facilities on a single campus.[1]

However, branch libraries entail a significant price in duplication of materials and diseconomies of scale. For these and other reasons, Rogers and Weber's reservations about branch libraries reflect the position of many academic librarians:

> Anyone who has worked in a general research library like the New York Public Library or the Library of Congress will appreciate the tremendous advantage of centralized collections. Anyone who has worked at the Harvard University Library sees the disadvantages of decentralization. Even in highly centralized research libraries, the deployment

of departments and collections over many acres of floor space and into annexes requires some duplication of materials and service expense. In the decentralized libraries, the frustrations of readers, the number of extra card catalogs to be maintained, the thinness of staff services, and the strains on the budget are severe.[2]

If there are to be branch libraries within a system--and in most cases branches do exist--the extremely difficult task of assigning subject literatures to branches must be undertaken. Variations in campus programs and geography make a single best solution impossible, just as historical and political factors may militate against even that solution which is best for a given institution. In general, however, the same kinds of issues will be raised wherever this important problem is addressed. In assigning subject literatures to branches, library administrators seek simultaneously to achieve three conflicting goals. They try to divide collections cleanly and unambiguously, minimizing duplication in holdings and patron uncertainty about where materials are located; to place within each branch mutually supporting literatures; and not to divide between libraries materials which are related and which are apt to be needed by the same persons.

The circulation data from VPI&SU may serve to demonstrate the difficulty of attaining these goals as well as to suggest lines of division which might optimize the assignment of subject collections. While the circulation data do show that most use varies predictably with the specialized fields of patrons, they also show a high incidence of cross-disciplinary use, both that which might be considered predictable and that which appears to be wholly idiosyncratic. Evidence of such extensive cross-disciplinary reading can only discourage the hope that collections can be distributed in such a way as to promote the convenience of some patrons without introducing serious problems for others. The use of library materials across disciplinary boundaries appears to exceed greatly the incidence of cross-disciplinary citation, and in general the data suggest that it would be difficult at best to identify discrete groups of subject literatures which can be physically grouped without forcing a library either to drag along or to cut away many other strands of a single skein.

Some choices will present greater problems than others, of course, and with less reward. The data suggest that few actions could have greater costs or fewer benefits than to segregate the literature of any of the social sciences. Researchers and students in most of the social sciences rely heavily on the literatures of other social sciences and on materials in history and the humanities, so that the availability of even the best specialized facilities would leave many of their library needs unmet. On the other hand, materials in a given literature of the social sciences will be used extensively by other social scientists as well as by researchers in more remote fields, and these patrons will find specialized libraries in the social sciences a burden.

The lines among the major fields of science and between science and other traditions appear, however, to be clearer and to hold within them a larger number of dependent relationships among disciplines. The life sciences and their applied disciplines are reasonably independent of other literatures, while they form a cluster of literatures among which use covaries importantly. The physical sciences appear to comprise an almost equally discrete cluster. However, it would be necessary to include in any library for the physical sciences materials in engineering and other fields of technology, not so much because researchers in the physical sciences need these materials as because of the reverse pattern of dependency. If basic physical science literatures are to be grouped in specialized libraries, the data suggest that mathematics, physics, and chemistry may provide a reasonably coherent cluster of literatures. Mathematics and chemistry are not closely related, but physics is so closely tied to each of these literatures as to make it difficult to exclude any of the three.

Because materials in mathematics, physics, and chemistry are basic to much work in applied disciplines, such a constellation of literatures might entail a significant hardship for workers in technological fields. The data suggest that, in general, it would be difficult to isolate any individual literature or small group of literatures without introducing problems similar to those associated with libraries in the individual physical sciences. It may be that larger library clusters would disrupt normal reading patterns least, while achieving a reasonable economy of scale. For example, large science libraries would reflect the traffic among the various areas of science and in particular the role of chemistry as a bridge between the physical and life sciences. However, such libraries would still tend to frustrate both the interests of historians and other humanists in science as an object of study and the needs of civil engineers and others in applied sciences for materials outside of science.

Besides suggesting the broad outlines which might govern branch library structure in general, the VPI&SU circulation data may be useful in evaluating existing structures. Any such evaluation would of course rest on the assumption that patterns of use at VPI&SU are reasonably typical, an assumption which can be tested only by studies which would replicate the present one. To determine the patterns of branch library structure which prevail in research libraries, data on departmental and branch libraries were extracted from *The American Library Directory* for all academic libraries in the Association of Research Libraries (ARL). The library units represented in the directory were listed for each library.[3] These lists were then collated by type of library to determine the frequency with which various kinds of library units are found.

The listings reveal that specialized literatures in the humanities and social sciences (or those which would be *least successful* in grouping self-contained bodies of literatures) are extremely rare. Only two libraries in English and four in history were identified. Five branch libraries restricted to psychology exist among the 101 academic libraries in the ARL, along with one in political science. There are no branch libraries in sociology. On the other hand, libraries holding materials in large, multi-disciplinary areas, or those which would *most sucessfully* circumscribe mutually supporting literatures, are nearly as uncommon. Libraries in the life sciences or encompassing materials in the physical sciences and technology are rare. For example, there are only ten libraries in science and engineering or science and technology among the ARL members, and only seven with "life sciences" as part of their names.

Many of the larger branch libraries which are found reflect lines of collegiate structure. Medical libraries are almost ubiquitous. There are medical libraries in forty-one institutions and fifty-eight other libraries which combine medicine and some other field like veterinary medicine or which reflect specialized fields of medicine. In addition to the ten libraries in science and engineering, there are forty-five libraries in engineering, or with engineering as part of their name. The data would suggest that the existence of these libraries does not seriously inconvenience most patrons from other fields, but that without extensive duplicate purchasing they may not be able to provide the full range of scientific materials needed by engineers. There are thirty-one branch libraries in education, twenty-eight in architecture, and twenty-two in business, including libraries whose names reflect combinations of these and other disciplines. If the VPI&SU data are typical, the patrons of these libraries would still need fairly broad literatures outside of their specialties, while patrons from external disciplines would require materials housed in these facilities.

Most of the libraries which contain the literatures of individual subjects are in the physical sciences and in the fine arts. There are twenty-six libraries in mathematics, twenty-seven in chemistry, twenty-one in geology, and eighteen in physics. Many of these are relatively small departmental libraries which do not hold all materials in their associated literatures, but the circulation data would suggest that to the extent that they do hold these literatures exclusively, patrons from many other fields would require the materials they hold. Mathematicians would be most able to work with the literatures contained in their branch or departmental libraries, but chemists, physicists, and geologists would find only about half of the materials they need in their branches unless collection development was expanded substantially beyond specialized disciplinary boundaries. In addition to branch libraries specializing in these sciences, there are approximately thirty libraries which incorporate various combinations of the physical sciences and seven which encompass the physical sciences as a whole. The forty-seven libraries in music, seventeen in art, and nine in the fine arts reflect the relatively specialized interests of patrons in these fields but may serve to frustrate patrons in the broader humanistic fields such as literature, philosophy, or history.

Does Library Structure Affect Reading?

The circulation data suggest that cross-disciplinary reading is very extensive and that, as a consequence, the task of dividing subject collections among specialized libraries is extremely difficult. Nevertheless, branch libraries are a common phenomenon in colleges and universities. In view of the inconvenience that patrons experience when only a portion of the materials they need are held at a branch library and of what is known about the behavior of library patrons, often described by Mooer's "principle of least effort," it is natural to speculate whether the lines of division among subject literatures which library systems impose may not actively structure reader behavior. Could it be that where subject literatures are segregated along branch lines, multi-disciplinary reading is discouraged and reading preferences come to mirror the structure of library systems?

So far in the analysis the reading preferences of faculty and students have been interpreted as evidence of the inherent dependence of academic disciplines on subject literatures. With highly centralized library services at VPI&SU, patron behavior should not be constrained by library structure. However, the circulation data suggest that the presence of branch libraries in geology and in art and architecture may introduce an exception to this pattern of unfettered use. Faculty in art, architecture, and geology read relatively widely and do not appear to be reluctant to borrow materials from the main library. But the data on supportiveness show that two of these literatures--architecture and geology--are among the least widely read of all those studied. Only 22 percent of the books in architecture charged to the faculty were charged to faculty not in the College of Architecture, while 9 percent of the books in geology charged to faculty were held by members of departments other than geology. Materials in geology may not be intrinsically valuable to a broad variety of disciplines. Still, one might not ordinarily expect that this subject would account for only one of the 149 books charged to faculty and graduate students in the Department of Mining Engineering, as the data indicate to be the case. Brown found geology "basic for much of the research in mining engineering," and one must wonder why materials in geology are so little used by patrons in this field at VPI&SU.[4] Separate analyses showed that "Geology" and "Architecture" ranked third and tenth, respectively, among the 81 subject literatures in the average number of books charged to active borrowers, indicating perhaps that only those patrons with extensive interests in these literatures bother to visit the branches in which materials are held.

Comparisons between the photocopy data and Flynn's findings on the use of branch libraries at Pittsburgh also suggest the possibility that branch structure may channel patron behavior. Flynn found that only about 14 percent of the use of journals located at various science branch libraries at Pittsburgh could be attributed to users from outside the body of "primary users" as defined by department. The percentage of external use was especially low for materials in chemistry (5.7 percent) and in mathematics, where no journal use was recorded except that by patrons affiliated with the mathematics department. In the face of such a low incidence of use by outsiders, Flynn concluded:

> The relative lack of crossover among the clientele of the various libraries suggests that specialized centers, designed along disciplinary lines, are feasible in considering alternative methods of providing journals, e.g. through resource-sharing centers.[5]

Neither the circulation data nor the photocopy data from VPI&SU would suggest any such conclusion. For circulating materials, the findings on supportiveness indicate that the substantial majority of use of materials in physics, chemistry, and mathematics is by outsiders. Supportiveness scores cannot be reliably calculated for the photocopy data, which is most comparable with Flynn's data, because of the biases determining the representation of most departments. However, cross-disciplinary use, while less extensive than for monographs, was still very significant, even within the sciences. For example, when supportiveness scores were calculated for photocopied materials in mathematics (where the faculty account for a virtually identical share of circulation and photocopying, indicating that bias is probably within reasonable limits), 40.4 percent of the 168 requests for copies were found to have been made by outsiders. This finding compares to 0.0 percent external use at

Pittsburgh. This distinction and others like it suggest that the data which underlie Flynn's conclusions may be little more than an artifact of the structure of branch libraries at Pittsburgh.

While suggestive, neither the VPI&SU circulation data alone nor comparisons between the photocopy data and the Pittsburgh findings on journal use would be sufficient to demonstrate that library structure affects use. In order to bring more extensive data to bear on this issue and to allow controls for such variables as differences in the inherent literature needs of various disciplines, data were obtained from a second institution, the University of Nebraska at Lincoln. Nebraska's land-grant university, the University of Nebraska at Lincoln (UNL) shares VPI&SU's emphasis on the applied sciences. The universities are broadly similar in their structure, with each having colleges in architecture, agriculture, arts and sciences, business, education, engineering, and home economics. There are of course differences: Nebraska has a College of Law and a School of Journalism, which VPI&SU does not have, and has assigned veterinary medicine the status of a department, whereas this is a college at VPI&SU.

While Nebraska and VPI&SU are generally similar as institutions of higher education, their library systems differ markedly. Whereas VPI&SU has branch libraries in architecture and geology only, Nebraska has, in addition to these, branch libraries in chemistry, mathematics, physics, engineering, law, the life sciences, agriculture and home economics, and music. The University also operates a dentistry library as a branch, although the College of Dentistry is officially a part of the University of Nebraska Medical Center at Omaha. The University of Nebraska at Lincoln consists of two campuses approximately three miles apart. Libraries within the city campus are generally within a five-minute walk of one another. The Chemistry and Life Science Libraries are especially close, while the Engineering Library is somewhat more distant from Love Library (the largest library, holding most materials in the humanities and social sciences) than are the others. All libraries are on the city campus except for Thompson Library, which holds collections in agriculture and home economics, and the dentistry and law libraries. To promote access to library materials, two paging runs are made daily, delivering requested materials between Thompson and Love Libraries. Other branches participate in a delivery schedule which routes materials among them two or three times a week. Most academic units in the agricultural sciences are located on the east campus, along with their supporting laboratories.

The comparability between the institutions and the differences between their library systems make possible an empirical examination of the hypothesis that branch library structure affects patron behavior by reducing the extent of cross-disciplinary borrowing. To achieve such a comparison, patron records were obtained from UNL for faculty within selected disciplines. The data provided listings of all books held by these patrons in late October of 1982. A broad sampling of disciplines was selected, reflecting faculty in the humanities, social sciences, and business who would be expected to rely on the collections of Love Library, and also in departments which would tend to rely on branch collections. Departments were selected before the analysis of the VPI&SU data had begun, so that spurious results due to selective sampling and an attendant regression towards the mean could be avoided. Data were obtained from computer listings of the books charged to these faculty members, whose identities were suppressed. Nebraska controls circulation through the DataPhase system. Patron records provided by this system include call numbers for items in use. Patron records also list the library to which each borrowed item belongs.

Call numbers from these records were coded according to the subject breakdown applied to the VPI&SU data. The staff at Nebraska provided information indicating which libraries are the predominant sites for materials in each of the subject literatures used in the study, except of course for the subjects "VPI&SU" and "Unassociated Records," for which there are no counterparts at UNL. To achieve comparability of the data, the VPI&SU circulation data from October 28 were used, rather than the main data, gathered in May. The main part of the analysis consisted of comparisons between the two institutions of the extent to which faculty in given departments relied on the subject literatures associated with the libraries at UNL whose collections matched faculty interests. For example, comparisons between the two history departments were based on the extent to which each relied on those subjects primarily housed at Love Library, while comparisons between the mechanical engineering departments reflected the proportion of materials which were in the subjects held predominantly at UNL's Engineering Library. The matchings between departments and their literatures of greatest interest were based on the circulation records of faculty at both institutions. To base the pairings on either set of data alone would have invited spurious findings due to regression towards the mean.

In a number of cases, departments at one institution or another had to be combined or departments with variant names had to be considered equivalent, in order to make the UNL and VPI&SU data comparable.

Data for UNL's separate departments of sociology and anthropology were combined for comparisons with VPI&SU's sociology department, which is responsible for both disciplines. VPI&SU's biology department was compared to UNL's School of Life Sciences, which was formed by the merger of earlier UNL departments in botany, zoology, and microbiology. VPI&SU's Department of Management, Housing, and Family Development and UNL's Department of Human Development and Family, each a part of its parent institution's College of Home Economics, were considered equivalent, as were VPI&SU's Department of Clothing, Textiles, and Related Arts and UNL's Department of Textiles, Clothing, and Design, also units of the respective Colleges of Home Economics.

Not all of Nebraska's libraries use the DataPhase system. Branch libraries in law and mathematics rely on manual circulation systems. For this reason, all use of materials in the subjects "Mathematics and Statistics" and "Law" was excluded from circulation records at both institutions. To promote the greatest degree of comparability, those occasional books held in a DataPhase library at Nebraska which were in the subjects mainly associated with non-DataPhase libraries were excluded, since these subjects had been excluded *in toto* from the VPI&SU data. Use of materials in "Medicine" was also excluded, as these materials are divided among UNL's Love Library and its branches in the life sciences and in dentistry. The circulation data from VPI&SU on use of materials in the subjects "VPI&SU" and "Unassociated Records" were also excluded.

The Nebraska library system began using the Library of Congress classification system in 1964 and has converted many materials held in branch libraries to this scheme. However, significant Dewey collections remain, especially in Love Library. The use of these materials was also excluded from the data, chiefly because the subject scheme used at VPI&SU did not distinguish among Dewey classes. Because of this exclusion, 488 of the 3,561 books that fell into the Nebraska data were omitted from the comparisons. The assignment of Dewey collections to branch libraries at Nebraska is less distinct than that which governs the allocation of materials in the LC scheme, but the Nebraska staff did provide a rough breakdown of the assignments. A separate analysis revealed that faculty were more apt to use books in the Dewey classes associated with the branch libraries considered primary to their departments, compared to their use of endogenous materials classified in LC. Thus, any bias introduced by excluding the use of Dewey materials is probably conservative with respect to the hypothesis.

Since the patron listings from UNL designated the holding library for each book charged to a patron, it was possible to derive a frequency distribution of patrons according to the number of libraries from which they had borrowed materials, and to analyze these data according to the number of books in use. Table 52 presents such a matrix, showing the number of patrons who had materials charged from a given number of libraries, according to the extent of their borrowing. Most faculty borrowers at Nebraska had materials from one library only. Even those patrons with a large number of books in use tended to rely on a single library, at least for those materials in use when data were gathered. Of those patrons with over twenty books, 58.9 percent had obtained their materials from one library only, which was also true for seven of the eleven patrons with over fifty books. Some patrons were not deterred by the branch structure, however, as is shown by the faculty member with one book from each of four libraries.

Table 52. Number of Branches from Which Materials Are Borrowed, UNL

NUMBER OF BOOKS	NUMBER OF BRANCHES					
	1	**2**	**3**	**4**	**5**	**Total**
1	52	--	--	--	--	52
2	24	4	--	--	--	28
3	11	4	0	--	--	15
4	8	5	0	1	--	14
5	17	4	1	0	0	22
6-10	31	8	2	0	0	41
11-15	16	1	1	0	0	18
16-20	7	3	1	0	0	11
21-25	9	6	0	2	0	17
26-50	17	8	2	1	0	28
51-100	5	1	1	0	0	7
>100	2	2	0	0	0	4
TOTAL	199	46	8	4	0	257

The analysis treating the subject distribution of materials charged to faculty of the two institutions was restricted to those departments where faculty in each university had at least twenty-five books in circulation. Data for each of the twenty-two pairs of departments meeting this standard are presented in Table 53. For each department, the table lists the Nebraska library or libraries considered primary to faculty interests, the percentage of books in circulation belonging to the primary library (including all books excluded from the subject analysis), and the percentage of books that fell into the subject assigned to that library, first at Nebraska and then at VPI&SU. Thompson Library contains UNL's collections in agriculture and home economics. The names of other branch libraries indicate their primary collections.

Table 53. Use of Specialized Materials at UNL and VPI&SU

Dept. (UNL name)	Assigned Library(ies)	Books Charged from Library	UNL Books Charged within Subject (n)	VPI&SU Books Charged within Subject (n)
Account'g	Love	100.0%	100.0% (38)	87.8% (98)
Agronomy	Thompson	90.1%	36.2% (69)	34.3% (35)
Chemical Engineering	Chemistry and Engr.	76.1%	76.7% (43)	81.8% (55)
Chemistry	Chemistry	89.0%	53.1% (239)	57.0% (251)
Economics	Love	98.9%	94.1% (219)	97.2% (389)
Entomology	Thompson and Life Sci.	100.0%	92.9% (28)	56.4% (39)
Food Science	Thompson and Life Sci.	94.1%	68.4% (57)	22.9% (48)
Geography	Love	95.8%	78.0% (109)	88.5% (234)
History	Love	99.1%	98.3% (834)	85.1% (456)
Horticulture	Thompson	89.2%	64.1% (39)	46.8% (111)
Human Dev. and Family	Thompson and Love	100.0%	100.0% (37)	89.2% (93)
Life Science	Life Sci.	54.5%	78.8% (250)	73.2% (291)
Management	Love	98.3%	89.1% (46)	93.8% (192)
Marketing	Love	97.8%	95.2% (42)	92.8% (111)
Mech. Engr.	Engr.	91.2%	76.3% (139)	51.5% (297)
Philosophy	Love	97.9%	96.0% (151)	94.0% (84)
Poli. Sci.	Love	96.6%	96.9% (194)	91.9% (248)
Psychology	Love	95.8%	92.5% (53)	66.0% (103)
Soc. & Anthro.	Love	99.5%	98.3% (178)	93.2% (337)
Textiles, Clothing, and Design	Thompson and Love	93.1%	85.7% (28)	62.7% (110)
Theatre Arts	Love	86.0%	85.7% (35)	52.0% (25)
Vet. Sci.	Thompson and Life Sci.	98.4%	95.3% (86)	84.8% (158)

For seventeen of the twenty-two comparisons, faculty at Nebraska rely more narrowly on the literatures associated with their primary libraries than faculty at VPI&SU rely on those same literatures. There is a less than .01 probability that seventeen or more comparisons out of twenty-two would fall in the predicted direction, if results were random. Taken as a group then, the comparisons suggest a difference which is statistically significant at the .01 level. At Nebraska, a total of 2,538 out of 2,914 books not excluded because of subject or department were within the subjects associated with branches of primary interest to faculty. This distribution of 87.1 percent of use within branch libraries and 12.9 percent from outside branch literatures compares to 79.2 percent use of associated literatures and 20.8 percent of external literatures for the 3,765 eligible books at VPI&SU. Comparing the 20.8 percent to the 12.9 percent, it is apparent that materials from outside specialized literatures (as defined in the branch-to-subject matchings) account for over half again as much circulation (about 161 percent) at VPI&SU as at Nebraska.

With a difference this large, and with seventeen of twenty-two comparisons falling in the predicted direction, there appear to be strong grounds for concluding that the structure of branch libraries does channel patron behavior.[6] This finding corroborates Dougherty and Blomquist's conclusions from their study of branch library structure and the use of on-campus document delivery systems. Based on their analysis of branch collections and of use patterns reported by faculty patrons, Dougherty and Blomquist noted that patrons tended not to visit all libraries with potentially useful holdings and concluded that "the branch library structure may well have impeded an individual's access to all relevant materials."[7] They found that faculty who had access to a delivery service showed a high level of satisfaction, which would indicate that such services may well reduce the extent to which branch structures may channel reading.

Interestingly, the percentage of materials checked out from the main libraries of interest at Nebraska rather consistently exceeds the percentage of books within the assigned subjects. This difference indicates that librarians at the branches have purchased selected materials outside of their major subjects, or have succeeded in having these materials assigned to their collections. Dougherty and Blomquist also discovered that branch libraries tend to acquire materials outside of their stated subject coverage, a practice which in their opinion led to something of a misalignment among branches, their collections, and their patrons.[8] Together with the delivery service, such collection practices probably mitigate the channeling effect of branch libraries at Nebraska, but they apparently fall rather short of removing it altogether. It should, of course, be pointed out that a split campus presents very difficult problems for library administrators. While they may wish to centralize materials, to do so would entail significant hardships for academic units in more remote parts of the university.

The main point the data appear to demonstrate is that while branch libraries can support most needs for library materials (especially if they purchase selected materials outside of their primary subjects), their very existence may inevitably interfere with cross-disciplinary reading. The VPI&SU circulation data make it clear that cross-disciplinary reading is not sufficiently channeled or predictable to enable one to avoid this effect through even the most liberal policies for collecting materials outside of specialized branch literatures.

Chapter 7

Afterword

> It is perfectly possible, for instance . . . to learn by sorting the
> cards what books the doctors among the Library borrowers
> had read . . . how many detective stories were borrowed
> during a certain time, what non-fiction had been borrowed by
> boys of a stated age . . . The possibilities of obtaining
> information on 'who reads what' are so unlimited that
> Montclair librarians will probably need to guard against
> seeking curious bits of information or riding professional
> hobbies.[1]

Research libraries spend approximately $500 million annually in
support of instruction and research. It would be difficult to think of any
other business or service which devotes such substantial resources to an
enterprise the needs and desires of whose clients are so little understood.
In part this deficiency of information stems from the difficulty of
measuring library use: many library activities leave little if any material
record for analysis. Yet the inadequacy of knowledge about use, and even
more about the needs of users, is also attributable to a feeling of distaste
for and suspicion of anything that could be construed as "market
research." In an era of accountability academic administrators express
frustration about the vague bases of knowledge which govern library
policies, while some librarians fear that the availability of more specific
data could lead to a narrow "crackpot realism" (in the phrase of C.
Wright Mills) which would seek to optimize arbitrary definitions of costs
and benefits at the expense of the broader humanistic goals of the library
and of the academy.

While there may be legitimate grounds for such fears, it is becoming
clear that data on how library materials are used will become much more
extensive and detailed. The degree to which librarians participate in

collecting these data and are involved in the process of interpretation and evaluation will depend on their own actions. Librarians in most institutions sense that circulation traffic would increase significantly if popular materials not useful for research were purchased, but they have wisely resisted such collection profiles on the basis of their professional judgment. These judgments are respected, and there is no apparent reason to believe that administrators will not respect the opinions of librarians when more extensive data on use are available or to believe that policies will be dictated by use data without an intervening opportunity for values to be expressed and debated. To base library policies on use data alone would be to abrogate a serious professional responsibility.

To base policies on value judgments alone, or on value judgments and untested assumptions about use, is also irresponsible and invites a very inefficient deployment of resources, to the detriment of important institutional goals. The present study has sought to contribute to our knowledge of how library materials are used. In many respects it substantiates the findings of citation studies and allows greater confidence that these may serve as a basis for library decision making. The degree to which social scientists rely on a widely scattered literature and the relative independence of the physical and life sciences exemplify such points of agreement. But the study also suggests certain understandings of library use which are not as consistent with previous interpretations. The extent to which scientists and researchers in applied disciplines use library materials, especially those in the basic scientific literatures, and the great volume of cross-disciplinary use of subject literatures are among the more prominent findings which might not have been expected on the basis of previous work.

The results of the study have a number of implications for the most basic aspects of library policy. By showing the degree to which use patterns depend on the disciplinary affiliation of library users, the study suggests that library use studies will be generalizable only to a limited degree and that an understanding of use must be based on the particular characteristics and missions of local institutions. By showing that specialists and nonspecialists use materials differently, the results call for a re-examination of fund allocation approaches to collection development. By demonstrating the extent and nature of cross-disciplinary use and the effects of decentralization, the results call into question the scattering of library collections and suggest lines of division which might best govern the structure of library systems. The high volume of cross-disciplinary use of library materials which the data have shown suggest that strong central libraries may be a powerful centripetal counterforce to the tendency of academic disciplines to break into non-communicating specialties. Both the findings that specialists and nonspecialists approach literatures differently and that branch libraries appear to channel reading patterns provide a basis for arguing that, when library policies are set by client groups, the result may be private virtues which are public vices. Such an argument would support the role of professional librarians as the best trustees of collections and arbiters of conflicting interests within user communities.

The results of this study leave many questions unanswered, though they may help to focus these questions better. The particular patterns of cross-disciplinary use suggested by the data require replication in different settings, particularly because only such replication can establish the extent to which the data may reflect the specific orientations of VPI&SU's departments or may be generalizable. The possibilities for using statistical techniques to trace the landscape of interdisciplinary relationships have only been suggested here; further work along these lines could have exciting implications, both for librarianship and for the sociology of science. Certainly the conclusion that branch libraries channel patron behavior is one example of the need for further work. While it may provide welcome ammunition for library administrators, this finding has policy implications that are far too serious to allow its full acceptance without replication. Within the centralized library structure of VPI&SU, undergraduates use materials from outside their major fields for a substantial portion of their borrowing. It would be especially interesting to discover whether this least sophisticated and determined group of patrons reads as eclectically in a decentralized structure, or whether branch library structures may channel and perhaps narrow the undergraduate experience. On the other hand, one would not wish to condemn branch structures *in toto* without an evaluation of just how much the proximity of branches may raise overall library use and without a better estimate than is currently available of just how small a collection of basic periodicals and reference works would satisfy most research inquiries. It would also be interesting to learn whether the internal placement of subject literatures within centralized libraries may affect reading patterns, especially as collections are grouped around service units.

Replication and elaboration of the approach taken in this study will become increasingly manageable as automated systems continue to develop.[2] Data of the sort used in the present study can be gathered by the creation and use of relatively straightforward and modest computer programs which proceed serially through all patron records, comparing each book in use to a call number table, and incrementing the appropriate subject-related field in the output record. A number of standard statistical packages provide powerful and convenient tools for analyzing such data. If data which represent circulation activity over a period of time are preferred over a snapshot of books in use at a given time, it would be necessary to incorporate data collection into circulation programs and to allocate adequate storage for continuous observation of circulation activity.

It would not be necessary for a given system to contain information on patrons' disciplines in order for the present approach to be replicated. Instead, data taken from circulation records could be concatenated with data files which would link patron numbers or names to departmental affiliation. Such files could be created at modest expense with the assistance of staff in charge of university records. As has been pointed out, no data about patron affiliation would be required to replicate this study's approach to correlational analysis of the relationships among use in specified literatures.

On a more modest level, information about "who uses what" can be obtained from photocopy request forms, from book-paging forms, or from checkout slips used for manual circulation systems, though in all of these cases data collection will be more tedious and error-prone than with automated circulation systems. Any means of obtaining truly representative information about the use of periodicals according to the disciplines of users is likely to rely on a relatively laborious and expensive methodology. Yet the importance of obtaining information on how such a large share of library resources is used would undoubtedly justify the effort. The data from this study tend to indicate that the use of periodicals follows disciplinary lines more than does the use of monographs, though periodicals use is by no means totally predictable. Just how closely the use of periodicals follows disciplinary lines cannot be specified in this report, but it would be important to know this.

More ambitious projects than the present study can be conducted in libraries all or most of whose collections have been converted to the full MARC format. This would make it possible for format, language, and age of materials, and not simply subject, to be analyzed according to patron status and affiliation. Such an analyis would be particularly useful in helping to trace the relationship between the age of materials used and the correspondence between the user's discipline and the subject of materials. It appears that the less closely patron and material are related, the more likely materials are to be monographic; it may well be that even if an analysis is restricted to the use of monographs, the slowness of communications among fields would be such that older materials are used disproportionately by those from more remote fields. Analyses which added the dimensions of format, language, and age of materials would require great dexterity in the partitioning of data, as the number of variables being considered simultaneously would be so large that researchers would "run out of cases" with even the largest data bases unless they could aggregate subjects or other measures whenever necessary.

In the passage which opens this chapter, Quigley points to the possibilities which automated circulation systems allow for examining "who reads what." Now, forty-two years later, studies such as she suggested are even more feasible than they were in the days of computer cards. One does not know whether to be more embarrassed for Quigley's generation and its optimism or for one's own, which has made but poor advantage of the vast stores of information available about library use. If this study succeeds in encouraging an empirical frame of mind that takes untested assumptions about use as a challenge, it will have served its purpose.

Stability of the Data

Most library use studies have been based on circulation data gathered over a time period. This methodology allows confidence that findings will reflect overall use patterns and will be immune to fluctuations in use according to the academic calendar or other sources of variation. One-time samples of books in circulation are easier and less expensive to obtain but raise the issue of how representative findings will be. In order to assess the stability of the findings in this report, data drawn from VTLS on October 28, 1982 were analyzed and compared to the main data, drawn in May. Whereas the May data were gathered about one week before the end of VPI&SU's spring quarter, the October data were gathered in the middle of the fall quarter.

The three tables below represent the comparisons which were made between the May and the October data. In Table 54, the percentage of materials in use by each patron class is reported. Undergraduates accounted for a larger share of books in circulation in the spring, a finding that probably reflects their use of materials for term papers. Otherwise, the distributions of materials by patron category are quite similar.

In Table 55, the overall percentage of use by subject is compared for the two sets of data. The observed percentages are reported so that readers may make their own assessment of the stability of the data. The reported correlation of use across the subjects is extremely high and would appear to justify a high degree of confidence in the reliability of snapshot data. However, the correlation is high in part because of the wide range of variation in use across subjects, and it would be lower if subjects had been divided so that use across them would be more nearly equal. Chi-square tests were also applied to the comparison and the results establish conclusively that the May and October data represent dissimilar distributions. The large size of both samples and the change in the distribution of use according to patron category make it almost inevitable that chi-square would reveal a difference in use patterns. Possibly the fairest summary of what the two tests indicate is that while the correlations show a great similarity in the results, the chi-square test indicates that differences do exist.

Table 56 reports the correlations across the eighty-one subjects for faculty in one department chosen at random from each college or from each area of the College of Arts and Sciences. The sample was restricted to departments whose members had one hundred or more books in use in May. Again, the correlations indicate that patterns of use are very consistent across time. It should be noted that due to the relatively liberal circulation policies for faculty, a significant percentage of materials will be represented in both samples, and that this will tend to raise the correlations.

Table 54. Use by Patron Category, May vs. October

Patron Class	Percentage of Use in May	Percentage of Use in October
Faculty	25.0	28.6
Graduate Students	36.2	35.9
Undergraduates	33.0	27.9
Staff	1.6	2.1
Other	4.2	5.6
Number of Books	58,457	51,876

Table 55. Use of Subject Literatures, May vs. October

Subject	May Circ.	October Circ.
General	.13%	.11%
Philosophy	1.10	1.15
Psychology	2.50	2.69
Religion	1.18	1.07
Auxiliary Sciences of History	.25	.28
General World History	.42	.44
European History	.93	.81
British History	.56	.39
History: Asia, Africa, Oceania	.86	.69
General American History	.15	.28
General U.S. History	1.19	1.13
U.S. Local History	.69	.78
History: Other American Countries	.28	.20
Geography	.67	.70
Anthropology	.50	.51

(continued)

Table 55 (continued)

Subject	May Circ.	October Circ.
Recreation	1.49	1.76
General Social Sciences	.42	.47
Social Statistics	.35	.39
Economics	7.04	6.15
Business Administration	3.85	3.66
Sociology	5.79	5.44
Political Science	1.59	1.56
Law	1.24	1.06
Education	3.99	4.00
VPI&SU	.89	.93
Music	1.17	1.16
Arts	1.99	2.60
Architecture	1.73	2.43
Philology and Linguistics	.31	.30
Classics	.42	.40
Other Languages and Literatures	.24	.28
English Language	.19	.22
Slavic Language and Literature	.23	.15
General Literature	.81	.87
Drama	.43	.24
Film and Broadcast	.23	.25
French Literature	.30	.22
Italian Literature	.12	.11
Spanish and Portuguese Literature	.21	.22
English Literature	3.37	2.57
American Literature	3.34	2.86
German Literature	.37	.27
Unreclassified Fiction	.71	.77
Juvenile	.67	1.31
General Science	.59	.61
Mathematics and Statistics	4.93	5.67
Computer Science	1.48	1.69
Astronomy	.17	.26
Physics	2.38	2.77
Chemistry	1.88	2.20
Geology	1.07	.94
General Biology	1.40	1.18
Botany	.93	1.08
Zoology	.97	.88
Entomology	.23	.19
Anatomy and Physiology	1.74	1.48
Microbiology	.42	.48
Medicine	3.49	3.19
General Agriculture	.59	.72
Plant Culture	1.46	1.27
Forestry	.19	.38
Animal Culture	.67	.54
Veterinary Medicine	.34	.31
Fish and Wildlife	.31	.24
Civil Engineering	3.29	3.37
Environmental Engineering	1.03	.80
Construction Engineering	.74	.70
Mechanical Engineering	.87	1.00
Electrical Engineering	1.98	2.36
Mining Engineering	.39	.48

(continued)

Table 55 (continued)

	May Circ.	October Circ.
Metallurgy	.19	.15
Chemical Engineering	1.10	1.07
Manufactures	.57	.76
Home Economics	1.09	1.25
General Technology	2.90	3.03
Military and Naval Science	.49	.54
Books and Bibliography	.32	.26
Library Science	.15	.20
Government Documents	.94	.78
Other	.70	.70
Unassociated Records	3.12	2.63

correlation, May vs. October = .982, $p<.001$.
chi-square, May vs. October = 802.775, 80 d.f., $p<.001$.

Table 56. Correlations for Faculty Reading, May vs. October

Department	Correlation
Plant Pathology and Physiology	.903
Environmental and Urban Systems	.992
Management	.989
Curriculum and Instruction	.844
Industrial Engineering and Operations Reearch	.835
Management, Housing, and Family Development	.737
Foreign Languages	.927
Sociology	.977
Physics	.992
Veterinary Medicine	.958

APPENDIX **B**

Student Reading

Table 57. Materials Used by Graduate Students in Agriculture

Subject	Agri. Engr.	Agri. Econ.	Agron.	Animal Science	Ento.	Fish. & Wildlife	Forestry	Forest Prod.	Food Sci. & Tech.	Plant Physiol. & Pathol.	All Agri.
History	0.0%	0.5%	2.0%	1.0%	5.4%	0.6%	0.6%	2.2%	0.8%	0.6%	1.2%
Language and Lit.	0.9	0.0	2.4	3.4	6.7	0.6	1.9	4.8	2.4	3.0	2.7
Other Hum.	0.9	1.0	0.0	0.0	1.3	0.6	0.0	0.0	0.0	1.8	0.5
Econ/Bus.Admin.	0.9	58.3	9.6	0.5	0.7	0.6	19.8	3.9	0.0	0.6	10.1
Soc. Sci's.	0.9	12.3	3.6	1.5	1.3	9.4	16.0	2.2	0.8	1.2	6.2
Phys. Sci's.	23.7	8.3	14.1	5.9	8.7	7.0	6.4	34.5	5.6	4.1	11.3
(LIFE SCI'S.)	(14.9)	(9.3)	(48.6)	(82.0)	(67.1)	(52.6)	(36.1)	(7.9)	(60.0)	(76.9)	(47.3)
Gen. Biology	1.8	0.0	6.8	5.9	18.1	17.0	1.9	0.4	8.0	8.9	6.5
Botany	0.0	1.5	6.4	5.4	4.0	1.2	9.6	2.6	13.6	11.8	6.5
Zoology	0.0	0.5	0.0	2.0	2.0	9.9	0.0	0.0	0.0	6.5	2.2
Entomology	0.0	0.0	0.4	0.0	17.5	1.8	0.0	0.0	0.0	0.6	1.4
Anatomy and Physiology	1.8	0.0	0.8	25.9	0.7	1.2	0.3	0.4	15.2	1.8	6.4
Microbiology	0.0	0.0	2.4	1.0	0.0	0.0	0.0	0.0	13.6	3.0	1.6
Medicine	0.9	1.0	4.0	6.8	2.7	4.7	0.6	3.5	3.2	0.0	2.9
Gen. Agri.	1.8	0.0	16.9	12.2	0.7	1.2	6.7	0.4	0.0	2.4	4.6
Plant Cult.	6.1	1.5	9.2	2.9	20.1	1.8	4.5	0.4	5.6	36.1	7.8
Forestry	0.0	0.0	0.0	0.0	0.0	0.6	11.2	0.0	0.0	3.0	2.0
Animal Cult.	0.0	0.0	1.6	8.3	0.7	2.9	1.3	0.0	0.0	2.4	2.6
Vet. Med.	2.6	0.0	0.0	11.7	0.7	0.6	0.0	0.0	0.8	0.6	1.5
Fish and Wildlife	0.0	4.9	0.0	0.0	0.7	9.9	0.0	0.0	0.0	0.0	1.3
Technology	37.7	4.9	8.0	2.4	3.4	7.6	6.4	36.2	28.0	5.9	11.6
Other	20.2	5.4	11.7	3.4	5.4	21.1	12.8	8.3	2.4	5.9	9.0
Active Borrowers/ Eligible	14/25	25/46	32/55	32/75	26/52	22/67	41/87	22/35	15/27	28/57	310/648
No. Books	114	204	249	205	149	171	313	229	125	169	2,182

Table 58. Materials Used by Undergraduates in Agriculture

Subject	Agri. Econ.	Animal Sci.	Biochem. & Nutr.	Fish & Wildlife	Hort.	All Agri.
History	4.8%	3.7%	1.9%	7.4%	2.8%	4.6%
Language and Lit.	8.6	5.6	13.0	8.8	7.1	7.6
Other Hums.	6.7	4.5	8.3	2.1	3.5	3.4
Econ/Bus.Admin.	35.2	6.7	0.0	8.2	8.5	8.5
Social Sci's.	7.6	7.8	6.5	12.5	6.7	8.9
Phys. Sci's.	1.0	3.0	1.9	3.1	0.4	3.1
(LIFE SCI'S)	(24.8)	(50.2)	(60.2)	(30.5)	(58.7)	(42.8)
Gen. Biol.	1.0	2.6	15.7	4.7	1.1	3.5
Botany	0.0	1.9	0.0	1.4	2.5	1.3
Zoology	1.0	1.5	0.0	6.4	3.5	3.1
Entomology	1.0	0.7	0.0	0.0	3.2	0.8
Anatomy and Physiol.	0.0	6.0	24.1	0.6	0.0	3.1
Microbiol.	0.0	0.0	2.8	0.0	0.0	0.4
Medicine	0.0	1.5	15.7	0.8	0.0	2.5
Gen. Ag.	6.7	1.9	0.0	0.4	5.7	4.0
Plant Cult.	1.9	3.0	0.0	4.9	42.4	12.1
Forestry	0.0	0.0	0.0	4.3	0.0	1.5
Animal Cult.	9.5	27.1	1.9	0.6	0.4	7.1
Vet. Med.	0.0	4.1	0.0	0.6	0.0	0.9
Fish and Wildlife	3.8	0.0	0.0	6.0	0.0	2.6
Technology	1.0	6.7	5.6	14.0	6.7	9.8
Other	10.5	11.9	2.8	13.4	5.7	11.3
Active Borrowers/ Eligible	30/ 166	94/ 651	24/ 93	153/ 733	72/ 316	460/ 2,403
No. Books	105	269	108	514	283	1,574

Table 59. Materials Used by Graduate Students in Architecture

Subject	Arch.	Envir. Design & Plan.	Land- scape Arch.	Urban Affairs	Urban Design	Urban Plan.	All Arch.
History	4.0%	0.5%	9.2%	0.0%	0.0%	4.0%	3.6%
Lang. & Lit.	8.6	3.0	3.9	0.8	0.0	1.4	5.0
Other Hum.	19.1	18.3	13.7	1.6	4.9	2.8	12.9
Econ/Bus.Admin.	3.4	10.9	13.7	35.3	21.4	33.0	14.8
Social Sci's	4.4	18.8	19.6	37.7	31.1	31.6	17.0
Phys. Sci's.	0.6	11.4	2.0	0.0	5.8	2.1	2.5
Life Sci's.	3.6	1.0	13.1	13.1	0.0	2.1	4.2
Technology	14.8	5.0	5.2	0.0	1.9	11.6	10.5
Other	41.7	31.2	19.6	11.5	35.0	11.3	29.5
(Arch.)	(30.7)	(23.8)	(9.8)	(0.0)	(12.6)	(2.4)	(18.8)
Active Borrowers/ Eligible	116/ 170	8/ 10	7/ 9	8/ 19	6/ 10	34/ 56	179/ 274
No. Books	866	202	153	122	103	424	1,870

Table 60. Materials Used by Undergraduates in Architecture

Subject	Arch.	Bldg. Constr.	Land- scape Arch.	All Arch.
History	5.0%	3.2%	12.6%	6.0%
Language and Lit.	7.9	1.9	0.4	6.0
Other Hums.	21.0	0.0	1.3	15.4
Econ/Bus.Admin.	1.5	16.8	5.0	3.7
Social Sci's.	5.2	5.8	7.5	5.6
Phys. Sci's.	2.7	4.5	0.0	2.5
Life Sci's.	3.9	9.7	31.4	9.1
Technology	14.3	45.8	12.6	17.4
Other	38.7	12.3	29.3	34.3
(Arch.)	(31.6)	(2.6)	(9.6)	(24.7)
Active Borrowers/ Eligible	300/779	40/147	35/69	375/995
No. Books	1,030	155	239	1,424

Table 61. Materials Used by Graduate Students in Business

Subject	Acctg.	Bus. Admin.	Econ.	Mktg.	All Bus.
History	1.1%	2.2%	3.2%	0.0%	2.2%
Language and Lit.	7.3	2.6	4.7	1.8	3.5
Other Hums.	0.0	1.6	2.6	0.0	1.9
(Econ/Bus.Admin.)	(59.8)	(48.7)	(57.3)	(40.9)	(53.0)
Economics	21.8	25.8	46.4	10.9	32.4
Bus. Admin.	38.0	22.9	10.9	30.0	20.6
Social Sci's.	12.9	25.6	14.9	50.0	20.4
Phys. Sci's.	6.2	1.1	3.7	0.9	3.3
Life Sci's.	2.8	2.9	1.8	0.0	2.1
Technology	4.5	6.9	0.5	0.0	4.5
Other	5.6	8.4	11.4	6.4	9.2
Active Borrowers/ Eligible	26/68	85/258	37/67	6/10	175/444
No. Books	179	550	571	110	1,585

Table 62. Materials Used by Undergraduates in Business

Subject	Acct.	Econ.	Fin.	Gen. Bus.	Mgmt.	Mktg.	Public Adm.	All Bus.
History	6.0%	4.8%	7.0%	5.8%	4.7%	7.3%	9.2%	6.1%
Language and Lit.	15.5	21.4	9.5	27.0	14.0	16.5	1.5	18.7
Other Hums.	4.2	3.2	1.9	3.6	5.2	3.8	0.0	3.5
(Econ/Bus.Admin.)	(19.3)	(31.8)	(43.0)	(12.7)	(38.1)	(34.6)	(47.7)	(25.7)
Economics	5.8	25.4	11.1	3.6	22.7	11.8	36.9	10.6
Bus. Admin.	13.5	6.4	31.9	9.1	15.4	22.9	10.8	15.0
Social Scis	23.0	15.1	11.4	18.4	12.8	8.3	30.0	16.8
Phys. Scis	7.1	0.0	1.6	2.4	2.0	1.9	0.0	2.7
Life Scis	7.5	4.0	8.9	12.7	5.8	9.8	0.0	9.2
Technology	5.3	11.1	5.1	8.7	7.3	5.1	0.8	6.9
Other	12.2	8.7	11.6	8.9	10.2	12.7	10.8	10.4
Active Borrowers/ Eligible	143/ 990	29/ 110	88/ 478	357/ 2,329	110/ 603	105/ 634	16/ 82	848/ 5,226
No. Books	452	126	370	1,091	344	315	130	2,828

Table 63. Materials Used by Graduate Students in Education

Subject	Adult & Contin Educ.	Educ. Admin.	Jr. & Comm. Coll.	Curric. & Instr.	Health & Phys. Educ.	Educ. Res. & Eval.	Adm. & Super. Educ.	Stud. Personnel	Voc. Tech. Educ.	All Educ.
History	3.6%	2.5%	0.3%	2.6%	0.0%	4.1%	0.0%	1.1%	0.6%	1.6%
Language and Lit.	1.2	0.3	1.5	14.2	1.9	4.7	2.3	3.0	0.0	3.8
Other Hum.	6.5	0.0	0.9	6.7	3.3	2.9	0.8	0.4	0.6	2.4
Econ./Bus.Admin.	6.5	11.9	15.3	1.2	1.9	5.8	5.4	23.0	11.3	9.6
(SOC. SCI'S)	(67.5)	(72.8)	(69.5)	(60.6)	(21.8)	(68.0)	(83.7)	(55.6)	(50.0)	(60.6)
Psychology	5.3	2.5	9.1	14.4	3.8	8.1	7.0	14.8	5.9	8.3
Geography	0.0	0.0	0.0	1.9	0.5	0.0	0.0	0.0	0.0	0.4
Anthro.	0.6	0.0	0.0	1.7	0.0	1.2	0.0	1.1	0.3	0.6
Gen. Social Sci's.	3.6	2.2	1.5	0.7	0.0	3.5	0.8	0.0	0.3	1.3
Soc. Stats	0.6	0.6	0.3	0.0	0.0	3.5	3.1	0.7	2.2	1.0
Sociology	17.2	6.7	6.2	2.4	10.9	14.0	10.1	7.0	5.0	7.5
Poli. Sci.	3.0	4.7	0.0	0.7	0.0	0.0	6.2	0.0	0.0	1.4
Law	0.0	2.8	0.0	0.0	0.0	1.7	26.4	0.7	0.0	2.1
Education	37.3	53.3	52.5	38.7	6.6	36.1	30.2	31.1	36.3	38.1
Phys. Sci's	0.0	0.3	2.9	2.2	0.0	4.7	0.8	0.7	4.4	1.9
Life Sci's.	8.3	1.4	2.1	2.4	31.3	4.1	0.8	8.2	6.9	6.5
Technology	2.4	1.1	0.0	0.0	2.8	0.0	0.0	1.5	7.8	1.8
Other	4.1	9.7	7.6	10.1	37.0	5.8	6.2	6.7	18.4	11.9
Active Borrowers/ Eligible	18/48	32/117	21/58	53/159	35/72	12/21	15/41	36/99	33/115	255/730
No. Books	169	360	341	416	211	172	129	270	320	2,388

Table 64. Materials Used by Undergraduates in Education

Subject	Elem. Educ.	Secon. Phys. Educ.	All Educ.
History	2.5%	8.3%	4.7%
Language and Lit.	19.6	1.5	8.8
Other Hums.	3.2	0.0	2.6
Econ/Bus.Admin.	2.2	1.5	7.4
Social Sci's.	22.7	16.1	22.7
(Education)	(14.8)	(6.3)	(13.0)
Phys. Sci's.	1.9	0.0	2.5
Life Sci's.	17.0	10.7	16.0
Technology	3.2	7.3	9.9
Other	27.8	54.6	25.4
(Recreation)	(14.2)	(50.2)	(16.0)
Active Borrowers/ Eligible	72/401	54/170	275/1223
No. Books	317	205	1012

Table 65. Materials Used by Graduate Students in Engineering

Subject	Aerosp. & Oceans Engr.	Chem. Engr.	Civil Engr.	Elect. Engr.	Engr. Sci. & Mechanics	Indust. Engr. & Res. Oper.	Matls. Engr.	Mech. Engr.	Mining Engr.	All Engr.
History	0.7%	0.0%	2.5%	0.3%	0.5%	2.3%	0.7%	0.9%	0.0%	1.2%
Language and Lit.	1.6	5.3	1.2	4.0	0.6	2.2	0.0	2.2	0.9	2.1
Other Hums.	1.9	0.4	0.8	0.8	0.8	0.9	0.0	0.6	0.0	0.8
Econ/Bus. Admin.	1.0	1.8	12.9	1.1	0.3	18.9	0.0	0.3	13.3	7.1
Social Sci's.	1.3	1.1	9.0	1.5	0.3	5.7	0.0	1.3	3.5	3.5
(PHYS. SCI'S.)	(36.9)	(35.2)	(17.7)	(37.5)	(47.2)	(29.1)	(28.5)	(25.8)	(12.4)	(31.0)
Math/Stat	27.8	8.8	11.2	20.6	40.5	23.5	9.5	17.6	5.3	20.9
Comp. Sci.	2.9	1.8	1.4	9.4	0.2	4.9	0.0	0.3	3.5	3.2
Astronomy	0.3	0.0	0.5	0.2	0.3	0.0	0.0	0.0	0.0	0.2
Physics	4.9	5.3	2.5	7.4	5.6	0.7	8.8	5.7	0.0	4.2
Chemistry	0.7	19.4	1.4	0.0	0.8	0.0	10.2	2.2	2.7	2.4
Geology	0.3	0.0	0.7	0.0	0.0	0.0	0.0	0.0	0.9	0.2
Life Sci's.	2.6	8.8	3.5	1.7	3.3	2.9	2.2	6.6	2.7	3.8
(TECHNOLOGY)	(46.0)	(42.3)	(44.4)	(46.9)	(41.1)	(29.6)	(65.0)	(51.9)	(56.6)	(43.1)
Gen. Tech.	22.7	2.5	3.0	2.0	5.3	11.2	0.7	11.0	7.1	6.9
Civil Engr.	13.9	5.3	35.3	3.1	30.7	4.3	30.7	19.2	13.3	17.0
Env'al Engr.	0.3	0.4	3.9	0.0	0.0	0.1	0.0	0.6	0.0	1.9
Constr. Engr.	0.3	0.0	0.3	0.8	0.5	1.2	0.0	1.9	0.9	0.7
Mech. Engr.	5.5	0.0	0.8	2.5	3.2	2.0	0.7	11.0	0.9	2.7
Elec. Engr.	3.2	2.1	0.3	37.9	0.6	2.5	0.0	7.2	0.0	7.4
Mining Engr.	0.0	0.0	0.0	0.0	0.2	0.0	0.7	0.0	31.9	0.9
Metallurgy	0.0	0.0	0.0	0.0	0.0	0.0	13.9	0.6	0.0	0.5
Chem. Engr.	0.0	31.0	0.8	0.0	0.2	0.0	11.7	0.0	0.9	2.7
Manufactures	0.0	0.0	0.1	0.6	0.5	7.6	6.6	0.3	1.8	2.1
Home Econ.	0.0	1.1	0.1	0.0	0.2	0.8	0.0	0.0	0.0	0.3
Other	8.1	5.3	8.0	6.3	6.0	8.3	3.7	10.4	10.6	7.5
Active Borrowers/Eligible	36/62	34/58	66/124	77/168	58/99	78/118	16/22	52/89	11/30	444/803
No. Books	309	284	774	651	665	858	137	318	113	4,205

Table 66. Materials Used by Undergraduates in Engineering

Subject	Aerosp. & Oceans Engr.	Chem. Engr.	Civil Engr.	Elect. Engr.	Engr. Sci. & Mech.	Gen. Engr.	Indus. Engr. & Opers. Res.	Mat'ls. Engr.	Mech. Engr.	Mining Engr.	All Engr.
History	4.4%	2.9%	1.5%	3.0%	3.5%	8.2%	1.6%	0.7%	3.6%	17.4%	3.7%
Language and Lit	7.7	8.6	4.8	7.4	15.6	26.4	4.0	7.2	8.1	0.8	9.1
Other Hums.	7.7	1.8	2.2	5.5	2.3	5.3	4.0	0.0	4.6	1.7	4.2
Econ./Bus. Admin	2.0	0.5	17.9	3.0	1.7	1.8	40.6	1.3	4.6	2.5	9.8
Social Sci's	6.1	3.7	14.9	5.9	2.3	9.4	18.6	5.9	7.3	4.1	9.0
(PHYS. SCI'S)	(8.8)	(14.4)	(5.9)	(21.2)	(19.7)	(5.7)	(4.3)	(21.1)	(7.7)	(16.5)	(11.3)
Math/Stat	5.4	2.1	2.6	6.7	13.3	1.6	1.9	7.2	2.4	0.0	3.8
Comp. Sci.	0.3	1.1	0.4	4.5	4.1	2.1	1.2	0.7	0.9	7.4	2.0
Astro.	0.3	0.0	0.0	0.8	0.0	0.2	0.3	0.0	0.4	0.0	0.3
Physics	2.0	2.9	1.1	7.8	2.3	1.0	0.6	7.9	3.1	0.0	3.2
Chem.	0.7	8.4	0.0	0.9	0.0	0.8	0.2	5.3	0.7	9.1	1.4
Geology	0.0	0.0	1.8	0.5	0.0	0.0	0.2	0.0	0.3	0.8	0.6
Life Sci's.	3.0	6.3	2.4	4.5	22.0	6.6	4.5	9.9	7.8	0.8	6.1
(TECHNOLOGY)	(49.8)	(50.5)	(37.6)	(44.5)	(21.4)	(22.1)	(17.0)	(50.7)	(46.5)	(35.5)	(37.5)
General Tech.	39.4	1.1	6.8	5.0	4.1	8.0	3.1	0.0	7.0	3.3	7.3
Civil Engr.	3.4	2.1	16.4	7.4	9.8	5.3	2.0	11.2	12.5	5.0	7.7
Envil. Engr.	2.4	2.4	4.6	0.6	0.0	1.6	1.4	0.7	0.7	4.1	1.6
Constr. Engr.	0.0	0.0	4.2	0.5	0.6	0.4	3.9	0.0	4.1	0.0	1.9
Mech. Engr.	1.7	1.6	1.3	2.8	2.3	0.4	2.2	0.7	8.6	0.0	3.0
Elect. Engr.	2.4	2.1	2.0	27.0	2.9	3.1	1.2	4.0	7.0	3.3	8.0
Mining Engr.	0.0	2.9	0.4	0.0	0.0	0.0	0.2	0.0	1.4	17.4	1.1
Metallurgy	0.3	0.0	0.2	0.0	0.6	1.0	0.0	27.0	0.1	0.0	1.1
Chem. Engr.	0.0	38.5	0.2	0.4	0.6	2.3	0.2	7.2	4.2	2.5	4.8
Manufactures	0.0	0.0	0.0	0.6	0.0	0.0	2.0	0.0	0.4	0.0	0.5
Home Econ.	0.3	0.0	1.5	0.2	0.6	0.0	0.9	0.0	0.6	0.0	0.5
Other	10.4	11.3	12.9	5.1	11.6	14.3	5.4	3.3	9.8	20.7	9.4
Active Borrowers/Eligible	84/407	101/447	141/761	239/1335	40/157	195/1,204	128/454	31/109	233/1,250	30/147	1224/6,309
No. Books	297	382	458	848	173	488	646	152	806	121	4,383

Table 67. Materials Used by Graduate Students in Home Economics

Subject	Clothing Textiles, & Rel. Arts	Human Nutrit. & Foods	Mgt., Housing, & Family Develop.	All Home Econ.
History	13.2%	4.2%	3.8%	6.1%
Language and Lit.	1.8	1.9	0.0	0.9
Other Hums.	0.0	3.0	1.3	1.5
Econ/Bus. Admin.	6.6	8.7	6.1	6.9
Social Sci's.	31.3	11.3	59.2	39.5
Phys. Sci's.	2.2	6.0	0.6	2.5
Life Sci's.	5.7	45.3	17.8	22.5
Technology	28.6	14.0	2.3	11.7
Other	10.6	5.7	8.9	8.4
Active Borrowers/ Eligible	25/44	41/81	41/88	107/213
No. Books	227	265	473	965

Table 68. Materials Used by Undergraduates in Home Economics

Subject	Clothing, Textiles, & Rel. Arts	Human Nutrit. & Food	Mgt., Housing, & Family Develop.	All Home Econ.
History	5.7%	2.0%	2.2%	3.4%
Language and Lit.	11.9	7.1	4.0	8.0
Other Hum.	9.9	0.6	3.6	4.8
Econ/B.A.	12.2	10.5	19.3	13.5
Social Sci's.	21.5	5.1	30.2	18.0
Phys. Sci's.	1.7	0.3	0.0	0.7
Life Sci's.	5.7	35.6	12.4	18.5
Technology	21.8	33.3	12.7	23.3
Other	9.6	5.4	15.6	9.9
Active Borrowers/ Eligible	85/432	81/264	67/248	236/978
No. Books	353	351	275	984

Table 69. Materials Used by Graduate Students in the Humanities

Subject	Engl.	Hist.	Theatre Arts	All Hum.
History	5.0%	50.3%	10.2%	21.4%
Language and Lit.	79.1	2.8	53.6	48.8
Other Hums.	2.1	2.8	9.6	3.6
Econ/B.A.	0.0	5.9	1.2	2.2
Social Sci's.	1.4	15.6	11.5	7.9
Phys. Sci's.	0.4	0.8	0.0	0.5
Life Sci's.	4.8	0.0	1.8	2.7
Technology	1.6	2.2	2.4	1.9
Other	5.6	19.6	9.6	11.1
Active Borrowers/ Eligible	34/41	24/41	11/19	69/101
No. Books	517	358	166	1,041

Table 70. Materials Used by Undergraduates in the Humanities

Subject	Art	Comm.	Engl.	Gen. Arts & Scis.	Hist.	Lib. Arts & Scis.	Theatre Arts	All Hum.
History	5.6%	6.9%	4.5%	7.1%	45.8%	4.3%	5.8%	9.5%
Language and Lit	5.0	20.4	56.7	21.5	14.3	13.6	36.4	26.0
Other Hum	62.6	4.2	6.1	9.1	4.9	15.7	29.8	13.2
Econ/B.A.	0.0	16.9	3.5	6.6	3.5	13.6	1.7	7.1
Soc. Sci's.	3.9	21.0	13.1	20.8	13.3	24.3	11.6	17.4
Phys. Sci's	0.0	2.1	0.2	3.9	0.5	3.6	1.7	2.1
Life Sci's.	5.0	2.3	3.3	11.7	1.5	7.1	3.3	6.2
Technology	5.0	14.0	1.2	9.8	1.5	11.4	1.7	7.4
Other	12.9	12.3	11.5	9.7	14.8	6.4	8.3	11.1
Active Borrowers/								
Eligible	45/	133/	78/	258/	43/	40/	23/	674/
	129	575	205	1,194	159	124	58	2,601
No. Books	179	480	427	829	203	140	121	2,569

Table 71. Materials Used by Graduate Students in the Sciences

Subject	Chem.	Geol.	Math.	Micro.	Phys.	Stat.	Zoo.	All Sci.
History	0.9%	0.9%	2.3%	0.9%	0.0%	0.9%	0.9%	0.9%
Language and Lit.	3.1	2.1	3.3	4.6	2.7	10.2	0.3	3.5
Other Hum.	1.1	0.0	0.7	0.9	3.2	0.0	0.9	1.0
Econ/B.A.	1.3	0.0	4.6	0.9	0.7	4.5	1.9	1.8
Soc. Sci's.	1.8	1.6	4.6	1.9	2.0	7.5	4.4	3.2
(PHYS SCI)	(64.4)	(62.2)	(71.3)	(6.5)	(75.3)	(63.4)	(6.5)	(54.3)
Math/Stat	4.2	1.1	67.0	0.0	16.9	60.4	3.7	20.9
Comp Sci	0.2	0.5	0.7	0.0	0.2	3.0	0.6	0.7
Astro.	0.0	0.0	0.0	0.0	0.2	0.0	0.0	0.0
Physics	9.2	3.2	3.6	1.9	57.5	0.0	0.3	12.3
Chemistry	50.9	7.3	0.0	1.9	0.5	0.0	1.6	11.1
Geology	0.0	50.1	0.0	2.8	0.0	0.0	0.3	9.2
Life Sci's	3.3	4.6	0.3	75.9	0.7	7.2	59.8	16.4
Technology	18.6	5.0	8.9	1.9	9.1	2.7	10.0	9.2
Other	5.7	23.7	4.0	6.5	6.4	3.6	15.3	9.7
Active Borrowers/								
Eligible	71/	51/	33/	18/	28/	27/	38/	285/
	121	86	69	36	54	61	65	529
No. Books	458	439	303	108	409	333	321	2,473

Table 72. Materials Used by Undergraduates in the Sciences

Subject	Bio-chem.	Biol.	Chem.	Comp. Sci.	Geol.	Math.	Phys.	All Sci.
History	6.0%	4.2%	6.7%	4.7%	3.5%	5.0%	16.8%	5.3%
Language and Lit.	13.9	16.2	14.8	19.1	20.6	20.5	15.8	16.8
Other Hums.	6.6	6.0	16.6	6.4	5.0	3.5	8.9	7.1
Econ./B.A.	2.7	3.0	0.9	5.8	5.0	9.5	2.0	3.9
Soc. Sci's.	9.3	10.9	4.0	14.6	5.0	14.5	10.9	10.2
(PHYS SCI)	(17.2)	(2.9)	(23.3)	(28.7)	(23.1)	(24.0)	(16.8)	(15.8)
Math/Stat	1.3	0.0	0.5	9.7	1.5	17.5	0.0	3.7
Computer Sci.	7.3	0.0	0.0	17.1	0.0	4.0	5.0	4.0
Astro.	0.0	0.2	0.0	0.0	0.0	1.5	2.0	0.4
Physics	4.0	0.9	4.5	0.6	0.0	1.0	9.9	1.8
Chem.	4.6	1.3	17.9	0.3	1.0	0.0	0.0	2.8
Geol.	0.0	0.5	0.5	1.1	20.6	0.0	0.0	3.2
Life Sci's.	25.8	35.3	9.0	7.5	6.0	7.5	6.9	20.2
Technology	9.3	8.8	14.8	7.2	9.6	9.5	12.9	9.3
Other	9.3	12.7	9.9	6.1	22.1	6.0	8.9	11.5
Active Borrowers/ Eligible	55/ 240	234/ 1,102	64/ 261	126/ 744	74/ 259	53/ 265	34/ 169	657/ 3,152
No. Books	151	898	223	362	199	200	101	2,207

Table 73. Materials Used by Graduate Students in the Social Sciences

Subject	Geog.	Poli. Sci.	Psych.	Soc.	All Soc. Sci.
History	11.3%	11.5%	0.0%	2.7%	5.1%
Language and Lit.	0.6	0.9	4.3	1.4	2.2
Other Hums.	1.9	1.8	0.9	12.3	4.5
(ECON./B.A.)	(15.0)	(21.5)	(7.9)	(21.4)	(16.0)
Economics	9.4	20.0	4.5	20.8	13.6
Bus. Admin.	5.6	1.5	3.4	0.6	2.4
(SOCIAL SCI.)	(41.9)	(56.1)	(44.7)	(49.3)	(48.5)
Psychology	0.0	0.3	29.0	2.2	10.6
Geography	19.4	0.0	0.0	0.0	2.4
Anthro.	0.0	0.6	0.0	3.6	1.2
Gen. Social Sci's.	0.0	1.5	1.4	1.6	1.3
Soc. Stats.	0.6	0.3	2.5	1.6	1.5
Sociology	6.9	16.7	9.0	34.8	17.9
Poli. Sci.	10.6	33.0	0.0	2.2	10.3
Law	2.5	3.3	1.1	1.6	2.0
Education	1.9	0.3	1.8	1.6	1.4
Phys. Sci's.	3.8	0.0	1.1	2.7	1.6
Life Sci's.	5.6	0.3	32.6	3.0	12.8
Technology	7.5	3.0	1.8	2.5	3.0
Other	12.5	4.9	6.7	4.7	6.4
Active Borrowers/ Eligible	12/16	17/32	56/105	25/40	110/193
No. Books	160	330	445	365	1,300

Table 74. Materials Used by Undergraduates in the Social Sciences

Subject	Econ.	Geog.	Poli. Sci.	Psych.	Soc.	Urban Affs.	All Soc. Sci.
History	2.3%	25.2%	12.9%	5.2%	6.4%	3.2%	10.2%
Language and Lit.	4.6	8.7	17.4	11.0	8.3	9.7	11.9
Other Hums.	0.8	1.7	6.8	6.9	4.5	4.8	5.5
(ECON./B.A.)	(37.4)	(11.3)	(18.5)	(8.3)	(10.5)	(28.5)	(17.1)
Econ.	29.0	8.7	14.6	5.2	7.1	24.2	13.2
Bus. Ad.	8.4	2.6	3.9	3.0	3.4	4.3	3.9
(SOC. SCI.)	(19.9)	(30.4)	(30.4)	(47.4)	(50.0)	(32.8)	(35.7)
Psych.	2.3	5.2	3.2	10.7	5.6	0.5	4.8
Geog.	0.0	15.7	0.3	0.0	0.0	6.5	1.8
Anthro.	0.0	1.7	0.0	0.6	2.6	0.0	0.6
Gen. Soc. Sci.	0.0	0.0	0.0	0.0	0.0	1.1	0.1
Soc. Stats.	0.0	0.0	0.2	0.0	0.0	0.5	0.1
Sociol.	9.9	7.8	8.5	33.3	35.3	19.4	18.8
Poli Sci	4.6	0.0	8.7	0.8	0.8	1.1	4.0
Law	3.1	0.0	4.6	0.6	2.3	3.2	2.6
Education	0.0	0.0	4.9	1.4	3.4	0.5	2.9
Phys. Sci's.	9.2	4.4	2.2	1.4	3.4	0.5	2.6
Life Sci's.	14.5	1.7	2.7	13.0	9.4	4.3	6.7
Technology	6.1	2.6	1.9	1.1	2.3	7.5	2.8
Other	5.3	13.9	7.1	5.8	5.3	8.6	7.5
Active Borrowers/							
Eligible	33/	26/	121/	89/	52/	41/	384/
	82	58	415	380	180	110	1,277
No. Books	131	115	588	363	266	186	1,739

NOTE: "Economics" is a program offering of the College of Arts and Sciences; a program with the same name exists in Business, as well.

Use of Grouped Subjects
According to Patron Category

Table 75. Use of Materials in Grouped Subjects by Patron Category

Subject	Fac.	Graduate	Under-grad.	Staff	Unaffil-iated	All Patrons
History	6.9%	3.1%	6.0%	7.0%	8.9%	5.3%
Language and Lit.	14.7	5.6	13.6	12.8	15.7	11.0
Other Hums.	8.0	2.6	6.5	4.7	6.3	5.4
Econ/B.A.	9.0	12.2	11.4	6.6	8.4	10.9
Soc. Sci's.	14.1	20.9	14.8	12.0	21.0	17.1
Phys. Sci's.	14.1	16.9	6.0	5.9	4.1	11.9
Life Sci's.	12.5	12.3	12.8	17.9	16.5	12.8
Technology	9.9	15.6	16.1	18.6	10.4	14.1
Other	10.9	10.8	12.8	14.5	8.7	11.4

Notes

Chapter 1

[1]Henry Small, "Co-Citation in the Scientific Literature: A New Measure of the Relationship between Two Documents," *Journal of the American Society for Information Science* 24 (July-August 1973): 265-69; and Derek J. de Solla Price, "Networks of Scientific Papers," *Science* 149 (30 July 1965): 510-15.

[2]Eugene Garfield, "ISI Is Now Helping to Bridge the Three (Not Two) Cultures," in *Essays of an Information Scientist,* vol. 3 1977-78 (Philadelphia: ISI Press, 1980), pp. 434-39; Derek J. de Solla Price, "Is Technology Historically Independent of Science? A Study in Statistical Historiography," *Technology and Culture* 6 (1965): 553-68; Penelope Earle and Brian Vickery, "Subject Relations in Science/Technology Literature," *ASLIB Proceedings* 21 (June 1969): 237-43; and Norman W. Storer, "Relations among Scientific Disciplines," in *The Social Contexts of Research,* ed. Saad Z. Nagi and Ronald G. Corwin (New York: Wiley Interscience, 1972), pp. 229-68.

[3]Michael Mulkay, "The Sociology of Science in the West," *Current Sociology* 28 (Winter 1980): 1-116.

[4]Robert N. Broadus, "Use Studies of Library Collections," *Library Resources and Technical Services* 24 (Fall 1980): 317-24.

[5]Herman H. Fussler and Julian L. Simon, *Patterns in the Use of Books in Large Research Libraries* (Chicago: Univ. of Chicago Pr., 1969); Stephen Bulick, William N. Sabor, and Roger R. Flynn, "Circulation and In-House Use of Books," in *Use of Library Materials: The University of Pittsburgh Study,* ed. Allen Kent (New York: Marcel Dekker, 1979), pp. 9-56; and William E. McGrath, "Correlating the Subjects of Books Taken out of and Books Used within an Open-Stack Library," *College and Research Libraries* 32 (July 1971): 280-85.

[6]McGrath, "Correlating the Subjects," p. 282.

[7]George A. Jenks, "Circulation and Its Relationship to the Book Collection and Academic Departments," *College and Research Libraries* 37 (March 1976): 145-52.

[8]William E. McGrath, Donald J. Simon, and Evelyn Bullard, "Ethnocentricity and Cross-Disciplinary Circulation," *College and Research Libraries* 40 (November 1979): 511-18.

Chapter 2

[1]Charles Harvey Brown, *Scientific Serials,* ACRL Monograph no. 16 (Chicago: Association of College and Research Libraries, 1956), p. 28; and Penelope Earle and Brian Vickery, "Subject Relations in Science/Technology Literature," *ASLIB Proceedings* 21 (June 1969): 237-43.

[2]Harry M. Kriz, "Subscriptions vs. Books in a Constant Dollar Budget," *College and Research Libraries* 39 (March 1978): 105-109; and Donald G. Marquis and Thomas J. Allen, "Communication Patterns in Applied Technology," *American Psychologist* 21 (November 1966): 1052-60.

[3]Robert N. Broadus, "An Analysis of Faculty Circulation in a University Library," *College and Research Libraries* 24 (July 1963): 323-25.

[4]Miriam A. Drake, *Libraries and Audio-Visual Center Cost Allocation Study* (RDU 76-02); West Lafayette, Ind.: Purdue University Libraries and Audio-Visual Center, 1976). Available as ERIC document 125566.

[5]The unpredictability of subject literatures purchased from subject-related accounts is discussed in Jacob Cohen, "The Economics of Materials' Use," in *Use of Library Materials: The University of Pittsburgh Study,* ed. Allen Kent (New York: Marcel Dekker, 1979), p. 126.

[6]Michael K. Buckland, *Book Availability and the Library User* (New York: Pergamon Press, 1975).

[7]Because government documents are entered into VTLS only as they circulate, they have a greater chance than other classes of materials to be represented as unassociated records in this study. Based on the inspection of a sample of government documents being returned to circulation and the observation that use of government documents and unassociated records tends not to covary across departments, it seems safe to conclude that the use of government documents is understated by at most the degree to which the shelf list measurement understated holdings.

[8]Cohen, "Economics of Materials' Use," p. 131; and George A. Jenks, "Circulation and Its Relationship to the Book Collection and Academic Departments," *College and Research Libraries* 37 (March 1976): 145-52.

[9]Herman H. Fussler and Julian L. Simon, *Patterns in the Use of Books in Large Research Libraries* (Chicago: Univ. of Chicago Pr., 1969), p. 66.

[10]The distinction between whether collection development is "supply-determined" or "demand-determined" is made in Cohen, "Economics of Materials' Use," p. 134.

[11]McGrath, "Correlating the Subjects of Books Taken out of and Books Used within an Open-Stack Library," *College and Research Libraries* 32 (July 1971): 280-85.

Chapter 3

[1]Herman H. Fussler, "Characteristics of the Research Literature Used by Chemists and Physicists in the United States," part 2, *Library Quarterly* 19 (April 1949): 140.

[2]Board of Governors of the National Enquiry, *Scholarly Communication: The Report of the National Enquiry* (Baltimore: The John Hopkins Univ. Pr., 1979).

[3]James C. Baughman, "A Structural Analysis of the Literature of Sociology," *Library Quarterly* 44 (October 1974): 293; William A. Satariano, "Journal Use in Sociology: Citation Analysis versus Readership Patterns," *Library Quarterly* 48 (July 1978): 293-300; Pauline A. Scales, "Citation Analyses as Indicators of the Use of Serials: A Comparison of Ranked Title Lists Produced by Citation Counting and from Use Data," *Journal of Documentation* 32 (March 1976): 17-25; and Margaret A. Nothiesen, "A Study of the Use of Serials at the John Crerar Library" (Master's thesis, University of Chicago, 1960).

[4]Penelope Earle and Brian Vickery, "Subject Relations in Science/Technology Literature," *ASLIB Proceedings* 21 (June 1969): 237-243.

[5]Robert N. Broadus, "A Citation Study for Sociology," *American Sociologist* 2 (1967): 19-20.

[6]Earle and Vickery, "Subject Relations in Science," p. 243.

[7]*Ibid.*

132   *Notes*

[8]Herman H. Fussler, "Characteristics of the Research Literature Used by Chemists and Physicists in the United States," *Library Quarterly* 19 (January 1949): 28; and Roger R. Flynn, "Use of Journals," in *Use of Library Materials: The University of Pittsburgh Study,* ed. Allen Kent (New York: Marcel Dekker, 1979), p. 98.

[9]Norman W. Storer, "Relations among Scientific Disciplines," in *The Social Contexts of Reserch,* ed. Saad Z. Nagi and Ronald G. Corwin (New York: Wiley Interscience, 1972), p. 258.

[10]Charles Harvey Brown, *Scientific Serials,* ACRL Monograph no. 16 (Chicago: Association of College and Research Libraries, 1956), p. 105; and Earle and Vickery, "Subject Relations in Science," p. 243.

[11]Earle and Vickery, "Subject Relations in Science," pp. 239-40.

[12]Robert S. Daniel, "Psychology," *Library Trends* 15 (April 1967): 670-84; and Earle and Vickery, "Subject Relations in Science," p. 239.

[13]Francis Narin, Mark Carpenter, and Nancy C. Berlt, "Interrelationships of Scientific Journals," *Journal of the American Society for Information Science* 23 (Sept.-Oct. 1972): 323-31.

[14]Donald T. Campbell, "Ethnocentrism of Disciplines and the Fish-Scale Model of Omniscience," in *Interdisciplinary Relationships in the Social Sciences,* ed. Muzafer Sherif and Carolyn W. Sherif (Chicago: Aldine, 1969), pp. 328-48.

[15]Earle and Vickery, "Subject Relations in Science," p. 243.

[16]Derek J. de Solla Price, "Is Technology Historically Independent of Science? A Study in Statistical Historiography," *Technology and Culture* 6 (1965): 554; and Illinois Institute of Technology Research, "Technology in Retrospect and Critical Events in Science," Vol. I (1968).

[17]Earle and Vickery, "Subject Relations in Science," p. 243.

[18]Price, "Is Technology Historically Independent of Science?"

[19]Marvin W. Mikesell, "The Borderlands of Geography as a Social Science," in *Interdisciplinary Relationships in the Social Sciences,* ed. Muzafer Sherif and Carolyn W. Sherif (Chicago: Aldine, 1969), p. 240.

[20]D.R. Stoddart, "Growth and Structure of Geography," *Transactions and Papers of the Institute of British Geographers,* publication no. 46 (1967): 1-19.

[21]Mikesell, "Borderlands of Geography," p. 232.

[22]Penelope Earle and Brian Vickery, "Social Science Literature Use in the U. K. as Indicated by Citations," *Journal of Documentation* 25 (June 1969): 123-41; and Robert Goehlert, "Periodical Use in an Academic Library: A Study of Economists and Political Scientists," *Special Libraries* 69 (February 1978): 51-60.

[23]Robert S. Daniel, "Psychology," *Library Trends* 15 (April 1967): 670-84.

[24]Storer, "Relations among Scientific Disciplines," p. 258.

[25]Baughman, "A Structural Analysis"; and Satariano, "Journal Use in Sociology."

[26]Satariano, "Journal Use in Sociology"; and Mark Jay Oromaner, "The Most Cited Sociologists: An Analysis of Introductory Text Citations," *American Sociologist* 3 (May 1968): 124-26.

[27]Broadus, "A Citation Study for Sociology,"

[28]Thorstein Veblen, *The Engineers and the Price System* (New York: B. W. Huebsch, 1921).

[29]Department of Education and Science--Committee on Social Studies, *Report of the Committee on Social Studies* (The Heyworth Report) (London: H.M.S.O., 1965). Quoted in J. M. Brittain, *Information and Its Users* (New York: Wiley Interscience, 1970), p. 66.

[30]Robert N. Broadus, "The Literature of the Social Sciences: A Survey of Citation Studies," *International Social Science Journal* 23 (1971): 236-43; and Daniel, "Psychology."

[31]Charles J. Popovich, "The Characteristics of a Collection for Research in Business/Management," *College and Research Libraries* 39 (March 1978): 110-17.

[32]George A. Jenks, "Circulation and Its Relationship to the Book Collection and Academic Departments," *College and Research Libraries* 37 (March 1976): 145-52.

[33]Board of Governors of the National Enquiry, *Scholarly Communication*, p. 45.

[34]William E. McGrath, Donald J. Simon, and Evelyn Bullard, "Ethnocentricity and Cross-Disciplinary Circulation," *College and Research Libraries* 40 (November 1979): 511-18.

[35]Paul Metz, "The Use of the General Collection in the Library of Congress," *Library Quarterly* 49 (October 1979): 415-34.

[36]Miriam A. Drake, "Attribution of Library Costs," *College and Research Libraries* 38 (November 1977): 514-19.

[37]Flynn, "Use of Journals," p. 82.

[38]Brown, *Scientific Serials,* p. 93; and Earle and Vickery, "Social Science Literature Use," p. 129.

[39]McGrath, Simon, and Bullard, "Ethnocentricity."

[40]Harry Bach, "Why Allocate?" *Library Resources and Technical Services* 8 (Spring 1964): 161-65.

Chapter 4

[1]Board of Governors of the National Enquiry, *Scholarly Communication: The Report of the National Enquiry* (Baltimore: The Johns Hopkins Univ. Pr., 1979), p. 46.

[2]William A. Satariano, "Journal Use in Sociology: Citation Analysis versus Readership Patterns," *Library Quarterly* 48 (July 1978): 293-300.

[3]Robert N. Broadus, "The Literature of the Social Sciences: A Survey of Citation Studies," *International Social Science Journal* 23 (1971): 238.

[4]Thomas S. Kuhn, *The Structure of Scientific Revolutions,* 2d. ed. enlarged, *International Encyclopedia of Unified Science,* vol. 2, no. 2. (Chicago: Univ. of Chicago Pr., 1970), pp. viii, 175.

[5]W. Y. Arms and C. R. Arms, "Cluster Analysis Used on Social Science Journal Citations," *Journal of Documentation* 34 (March 1978): 1-11.

[6]Donald T. Campbell, "Ethnocentrism of Disciplines and the Fish-Scale Model of Omniscience," in *Interdisciplinary Relationships in the Social Sciences,* ed. Muzafer Sherif and Carolyn W. Sherif (Chicago: Aldine, 1969), p. 331.

[7]Maurice B. Line, "Social Scientists' Information," *SSRC Newsletter* 3 (May 1968): 2-5. Quoted in J. M. Brittain, *Information and Its Users,* (New York: Wiley Interscience, 1970), p. 50.

[8]Diana Crane, *Invisible Colleges: Diffusion of Knowledge in Scientific Communities* (Chicago: Univ. of Chicago Pr., 1972), p. 93.

[9]Norman Storer, "Relations among Scientific Disciplines," in *The Social Contexts of Research,* ed. Saad Z. Nagi and Ronald G. Corwin (New York: Wiley Interscience, 1972), p. 237.

[10]Eugene Garfield, "ISI Is Now Helping to Bridge the Three (Not Two) Cultures," in *Essays of an Information Scientist,* vol. 3, 1977-78 (Philadelphia: ISI Press, 1980), pp. 434-39.

[11]Penelope Earle and Brian Vickery, "Social Science Literature Use in the U. K. as Indicated by Citations," *Journal of Documentation* 25 (June 1969): 123-41.

[12] *Ibid.,* p. 128.

[13]Donald G. Marquis and Thomas J. Allen, "Communication Patterns in Applied Technology," *American Psychologist* 21 (November 1966): 1052-60.

¹⁴Derek J. de Solla Price, "Is Technology Historically Independent of Science? A Study in Statistical Historiography," *Technology and Culture* 6 (1965): 553-68.

¹⁵Charles Harvey Brown, *Scientific Serials,* ACRL Monograph no. 16 (Chicago: Association of College and Research Libraries, 1956), p. 28.

¹⁶James C. Baughman, "Toward a Structural Approach to Collection Development," *College and Research Libraries* 38 (May 1977): 241-48.

¹⁷Derek J. de Solla Price, "The Revolution in Mapping of Science," in *Information Choices and Policies: Proceedings of the American Society for Information Science Annual Meeting* 16 (1979): 249-53.

¹⁸William E. McGrath, "Disciplinary Interdependence in University Students' Use of Books," in *Information Politics: Proceedings of the American Society for Information Science Annual Meeting:* 13 (1976), pt. 2, Full Papers. McGrath has since taken the promising approach of analyzing the similarities and differences among disciplines in terms of their use of subject literatures. See William E. McGrath, "Multidimensional Mapping of Book Circulation in a University Library," *College and Research Libraries* 44 (March 1983): 103-15.

¹⁹Tests of significance are sometimes omitted when data are available for an entire population, since sampling error is not possible in such a case. Significance tests are applied here in order to assess the extent to which relationships rest on a sufficient base to warrant theoretical interest and are likely to extend to a larger population of inference. A more extensive discussion of this methodological choice may be found in Hubert M. Blalock, Jr., *Social Statistics,* 2d ed (New York: McGraw Hill, 1972), pp. 238-39.

Chapter 5

¹Francis Narin, Mark Carpenter, and Nancy C. Berlt, "Interrelationships of Scientific Journals," *Journal of the American Society for Information Science* 23 (Sept.-Oct. 1972): 323-31.

²William E. McGrath, "Disciplinary Interdependence in University Students' Use of Books," in *Information Politics: Proceedings of the American Society for Information Science Annual Meeting* 13 (1976), pt. 2, Full Papers.

³*Ibid.*

⁴*Ibid.*

Chapter 6

¹Richard M. Dougherty and Laura L. Blomquist, *Improving Access to Library Resources: The Influence of Organization of Library Collections, and of User Attitudes Toward Innovative Services* (Metuchen, N.J.: Scarecrow, 1974).

²Rutherford D. Rogers and David C. Weber, *University Library Administration* (New York: H. W. Wilson, 1971), p. 73.

³*American Library Directory* 33d ed. (New York: R. R. Bowker, 1980).

⁴Charles Harvey Brown, *Scientific Serials,* ACRL Monograph no. 16 (Chicago: Association of College and Research Libraries, 1956), p. 105.

⁵Roger R. Flynn, "Use of Journals," in *Use of Library Materials: The University of Pittsburgh Study,* ed. Allen Kent (New York: Marcel Dekker, 1979), p. 98.

⁶The anonymous reader whose services were provided by the Council on Library Resources has pointed out that faculty patrons may borrow less from branch libraries because they know that collections are convenient and can easily be accessed when needed. If this is so, the observed contrast between use patterns at VPI&SU and at Nebraska would understate the extent to which branch structures channel reading. If, on the other hand,

patrons are more willing to borrow from a branch, it would not necessarily be true that their use of a central library is depressed in an absolute sense, and the conclusion would be called into question. However, such an argument would still not account for the apparent differences in the use of endogenous periodicals at Pittsburgh and at VPI&SU.

[7]Dougherty and Blomquist, *Improving Access to Library Resources,* p. 66.
[8]*Ibid.*

Chapter 7

[1]Margery C. Quigley, "Library Facts from IBM Cards," *Library Journal* 66 (December 1941): 1065-67, quoted by John Lubans, Jr. in "Systems Analysis, Machineable Circulation Data and Library Use Research," in *Reader in Library Systems Analysis,* ed. John Lubans, Jr. and Edward A. Chapman (Englewood, Col.: Microcard Editions Books, 1975), p. 422.

[2]Those libraries which have acquired the Virginia Tech Library System may contact the VPI&SU Center for Library Automation at Newman Library to obtain access to the programs that provide output data for replication of this study.

Bibliography

American Library Directory. 33d ed. New York: R.R. Bowker, 1980.

Arms, W. Y., and Arms, C. R. "Cluster Analyis Used on Social Science Journal Citations." *Journal of Documentation* 34 (March 1978): 1-11.

Bach, Harry. "Why Allocate?" *Library Resources and Technical Services* 8 (Spring 1964): 161-65.

Baughman, James C. "A Structural Analysis of the Literature of Sociology." *Library Quarterly* 44 (October 1974): 293-308.

_____ . "Toward a Structural Approach to Collection Development." *College and Research Libraries* 38 (May 1977): 241-48.

Blalock, Hubert M., Jr. *Social Statistics.* 2nd ed. New York: McGraw-Hill, 1972.

Board of Governors of the National Enquiry. *Scholarly Communication: The Report of the National Enquiry.* Baltimore: Johns Hopkins University Press, 1979.

Brittain, J. M. *Information and Its Users.* New York: Wiley Interscience, 1970.

Broadus, Robert N. "An Analysis of Faculty Circulation in a University Library." *College and Research Libraries* 24 (July 1963): 323-25.

_____ . "A Citation Study for Sociology." *American Sociologist* 2 (1967): 19-20.

_____ . "The Literature of the Social Sciences: A Survey of Citation Studies." *International Social Science Journal* 23 (1971): 236-43.

_____ . "Use Studies of Library Collections." *Library Resources and Technical Services* 24 (Fall 1980): 317-24.

Brown, Charles Harvey. *Scientific Serials.* ACRL Monograph no. 16. Chicago: Association of College and Research Libraries, 1956.

Buckland, Michael H. *Book Availability and the Library User.* New York: Pergamon, 1975.

Bulick, Stephen; Sabor, William N.; and Flynn, Roger R. "Circulation and In-House Use of Books." In *Use of Library Materials: The University of Pittsburgh Study,* pp. 9-56. Edited by Allen Kent. New York: Marcel Dekker, 1979.

Campbell, Donald T. "Ethnocentrism of Disciplines and the Fish-Scale Model of Omniscience." In *Interdisciplinary Relationships in the Social Sciences,* pp. 328-48. Edited by Muzafer Sherif and Carolyn W. Sherif. Chicago: Aldine, 1969.

Cohen, Jacob. "The Economics of Materials' Use." In *Use of Library Materials: The University of Pittsburgh Study,* pp. 105-60. Edited by Allen Kent. New York: Marcel Dekker, 1979.

Crane, Diana. *Invisible Colleges: Diffusion of Knowledge in Scientific Communities.* Chicago: Univ. of Chicago Pr., 1972.

Daniel, Robert S. "Psychology." *Library Trends* 15 (April 1967): 670-84.

Department of Education and Science--Committee on Social Studies. *Report of the Committee on Social Studies* (The Heyworth Report). London: H.M.S.O., 1965. Quoted in J. M. Brittain, *Information and Its Users,* p. 66. New York: Wiley Interscience, 1970.

Dougherty, Richard M., and Blomquist, Laura L. *Improving Access to Library Resources: The Influence of Organization of Library Collections, and of User Attitudes Toward Innovative Services.* Metuchen, N.J.: Scarecrow, 1974.

Drake, Miriam A. *Libraries and Audio-Visual Center Cost Allocation Study* (RDU 76-02); West Lafayette, Ind.: Purdue University Libraries and Audio-Visual Center, 1976. Available as ERIC document 125566.

_____ . "Attribution of Library Costs." *College and Research Libraries* 38 (November 1977): 514-19.

Earle, Penelope, and Vickery, Brian. "Social Science Literature Use in the U. K. as Indicated by Citations." *Journal of Documentation* 25 (June 1969): 123-41.

_____ . "Subject Relations in Science/Technology Literature." *ASLIB Proceedings* 21 (June 1969): 237-43.

Flynn, Roger R. "Use of Journals." In *Use of Library Materials: The University of Pittsburgh Study,* pp. 57-104. Edited by Allen Kent. New York: Marcel Dekker, 1979.

Fussler, Herman H. "Characteristics of the Research Literature Used by Chemists and Physicists in the United States." *Library Quarterly* 19 (January 1949): 19-35.

_____ . "Characteristics of the Research Literature Used by Chemists and Physicists in the United States." Part 2. *Library Quarterly* 19 (April 1949): 119-43.

_____ , and Simon, Julian L. *Patterns in the Use of Books in Large Research Libraries.* Chicago: Univ. of Chicago Pr., 1969.

Garfield, Eugene. "ISI Is Now Helping to Bridge the Three (Not Two) Cultures." In *Essays of an Information Scientist,* pp. 434-39. Vol. 3, 1977-78. Philadelphia: ISI Press, 1980.

Goehlert, Robert. "Periodical Use in an Academic Library: A Study of Economists and Political Scientists." *Special Libraries* 69 (February 1978): 51-60.

Hindle, Anthony, and Buckland, Michael K. "In-Library Book Usage in Relation to Circulation." *Collection Management* 2 (Winter 1978): 265-77.

Illinois Institute of Technology Research Institute. "Technology in Retrospect and Critical Events in Science." Vol. 1. 1968.

Jenks, George A. "Circulation and Its Relationship to the Book Collection and Academic Departments." *College and Research Libraries* 37 (March 1976): 145-52.

Kriz, Harry M. "Subscriptions vs. Books in a Constant Dollar Budget." *College and Research Libraries* 39 (March 1978): 105-9.

Kuhn, Thomas S. *The Structure of Scientific Revolutions.* 2d ed., enlarged. *International Encyclopedia of Unified Science,* vol. 2, no. 2. Chicago: Univ. of Chicago Pr., 1970.

Line, Maurice B. "Social Scientists' Information." *SSRC Newsletter* 3 (May 1968): 2-5. Quoted in J. M. Brittain, *Information and Its Users,* p. 50. New York: Wiley Interscience, 1970.

McGrath, William E. "Correlating the Subjects Of Books Taken Out of and Books Used within an Open-Stack Library." *College and Research Libraries* 32 (July 1971): 280-85.

————— . "Disciplinary Interdependence in University Students' Use of Books." In *Information Politics: Proceedings of the American Society for Information Science Annual Meeting* 13 (1976). Part 2: Full Papers (microfiche).

————— . "Multidimensional Mapping of Book Circulation in a University Library." *College and Research Libraries* 44 (March 1983): 103-15.

————— , Simon, Donald J.; and Bullard, Evelyn. "Ethnocentricity and Cross-Disciplinary Circulation." *College and Research Libraries* 40 (November 1979): 511-18.

Marquis, Donald G., and Allen, Thomas J. "Communication Patterns in Applied Technology." *American Psychologist* 21 (November 1966): 1052-60.

Martyn, John. "Progress in Documentation." *Journal of Documentation* 31 (December 1975): 290-97.

Metz, Paul. "The Use of the General Collection in the Library of Congress." *Library Quarterly* 49 (October 1979): 415-34.

Mikesell, Marvin W. "The Borderlands of Geography as a Social Science." In *Interdisciplinary Relationships in the Social Sciences,* pp. 227-48. Edited by Muzafer Sherif and Carolyn W. Sherif. Chicago: Aldine, 1969.

Mulkay, Michael. "The Sociology of Science in the West." *Current Sociology* 28 (Winter 1980): 1-116.

Narin, Francis; Carpenter, Mark; and Berlt, Nancy C. "Interrelationships of Scientific Journals." *Journal of the American Society for Information Science* 23 (September-October 1972): 323-31.

Nothiesen, Margaret A. "A Study of the Use of Serials at the John Crerar Library." Master's thesis, University of Chicago, 1960.

Oromaner, Mark Jay. "The Most Cited Sociologists: An Analysis of Introductory Text Citations." *American Sociologist* 3 (May 1968): 124-26.

Popovich, Charles J. "The Characteristics of a Collection for Research in Business/Management." *College and Research Libraries* 39 (March 1978): 110-17.

Price, Derek J. de Solla. "Is Technology Historically Independent of Science? A Study in Statistical Historiography." *Technology and Culture* 6 (1965): 553-68.

———. "Networks of Scientific Papers." *Science* 149 (30 July 1965): 510-15.

———. "The Revolution in Mapping of Science." In *Information Choices and Policies: Proceedings of the American Society for Information Science Annual Meeting* 16 (1979): 249-53.

Price, Nancy, and Schiminovich, Samuel. "A Clustering Experiment: First Step towards a Computer-Generated Classification Scheme." *Information Storage and Retrieval* 4 (1968): 271-80.

Quigley, Margery C. "Library Facts from IBM Cards." *Library Journal* 66 (December 1941): 1065-67. Quoted in John Lubans, Jr. "Systems Analysis, Machineable Circulation Data and Library Use Research." In *Reader in Library Systems Analysis,* pp. 421-31. Edited by John Lubans, Jr. and Edward A. Chapman. Englewood, Col.: Microcard Editions Books, 1975.

Rogers, Rutherford D., and Weber, David C. *University Library Administration.* New York: H. W. Wilson, 1971.

Satariano, William A. "Journal Use in Sociology: Citation Analysis versus Readership Patterns." *Library Quarterly* 48 (July 1978): 293-300.

Scales, Pauline A. "Citation Analyses as Indicators of the Use of Serials: A Comparison of Ranked Title Lists Produced by Citation Counting and from Use Data." *Journal of Documentation* 32 (March 1976): 17-25.

Small, Henry. "Co-Citation in the Scientific Literature: A New Measure of the Relationship between Two Documents." *Journal of the American Society for Information Science* 24 (July-August 1973): 265-69.

———, and Griffith, Belver C. "The Structure of Scientific Literatures I: Identifying and Graphing Specialties." *Science Studies* 4 (1974): 17-40.

Stoddart, D. R. "Growth and Structure of Geography." *Transactions and Papers of the Institute of British Geographers,* publication no. 46 (1967): 1-19.

Storer, Norman W. "Relations among Scientific Disciplines." In *The Social Contexts of Research,* pp. 229-68. Edited by Saad Z. Nagi and Ronald G. Corwin. New York: Wiley Interscience, 1972.

Veblen, Thorstein. *The Engineers and the Price System.* New York: B. W. Huebsch, 1921.

Index

Agriculture, use by College of, 39-41
    118-119
Architecture, use by College of, 49-50,
    93-94, 119-120
Arms, W. Y., 66
Art, use by Department of, 47, 126
Association of Research Libraries
    (ARL), 98

Baughman, James C., 29, 43, 71
Bibliographic coupling, 2, 72
Biology, use by Department of, 34-35
Branch libraries, effects on library use,
    95, 99-106
    frequency of among ARL libraries,
    98-99
    problems and choices associated
    with, 95-97
Broadus, Robert N., 4, 14, 30, 44,
    51, 65
Brown, Charles Harvey, 13, 35-36,
    53, 71, 100
Buckland, Michael H., 19
Bucknell University Libraries, 19-22
Bulick, Stephen, 4
Business, use by College of, 45-46, 120

Campbell, Donald T., 4, 37, 66
Chemistry, use by Department of, 35,
    126-127
Chi-square tests, 60, 74
Citation studies, 2-3

and use studies compared, 29-30,
    44, 65, 68-69, 108
    see also specific disciplines for refer-
    ences to citation studies
Classification schemes, 71-72
Cocitation analysis, 2, 72
Cohen, Jacob, 20
Collection development, implications
    of study for, 59-63
Communications, use by Department
    of, 47-48, 126
Correlational analysis of relationships
    among disciplines, 71-79
Council on Library Resources, xiii
Crane, Diana, 67-68

Daniel, Robert S, 36, 43, 44
Delivery services, 106
Demand interference, 19
Demographic explanations of book
    use, 22, 26, 89-91
Dougherty, Richard M., 95, 106
Drake, Miriam A., 14, 50

Earle, Penelope, 3, 13, 30, 35, 36,
    38, 39, 43, 53, 68-70
Education, use by College of, 44-45,
    121-122
Engineering, use by College of, 37-39,
    62, 82-85, 91-92, 123-124
English, use by Department of, 48, 61,
    125-126

141